Bonsai

Pinus
parviflora

Bonsai

Jon Ardle

MITCHELL BEAZLEY

THE ROYAL HORTICULTURAL SOCIETY

Bonsai
Jon Ardle

First published in Great Britain in 2003 by Cassell Illustrated, an imprint
of Octopus Publishing Group Limited.
This edition published in 2008 in association with the Royal
Horticultural Society by Mitchell Beazley, an imprint of Octopus
Publishing Group Limited, 2–4 Heron Quays, London E14 4JP
An Hachette Livre UK Company
www.octopusbooks.co.uk

A CIP catalogue record for this book is available from the
British Library.

ISBN 978 1 84533 378 2

Commissioning Editor Camilla Stoddart
Designer Justin Hunt

Set in Bembo

Colour reproduction by Dot Gradations Ltd.
Printed and Bound by Toppan in China

RHS

Contents

The heavy lower trunk of the white pine, Pinus parviflora, *on p. 2, gives the tree great presence, but probably indicates that it was grafted just below the first branches onto a more vigorous black pine,* Pinus thunbergii, *rootstock.*

INTRODUCTION

There is an undefinable 'something' about bonsai that powerfully fascinates some, and repels others just as strongly; few viewers are left ambivalent. One of the greatest ironies is that good bonsai are images of trees from nature in miniature, and are carefully trained to look like scaled-down versions of wild trees: to dismiss them as 'unnatural', or 'artificial', is to completely miss the ethos at the heart of the art form.

I would argue that, at its best, bonsai is undoubtedly an art form, but one like no other, for it is practised on living organisms. As such, unlike other pieces of art, bonsai are never 'finished' in the sense a painting or a piece of sculpture is. Because they are living, bonsai require constant attention, particularly in meeting their needs for water and nutrients and, as they are continually growing, they require regular pruning to keep their shape. Although training bonsai can therefore be seen as a kind of sculpture, since they are by definition three-dimensional, there is a fourth dimension to be taken into account – that of time, and this makes bonsai unique.

If bonsai is an art form, it can still be enjoyed on a number of levels. Not everyone who enjoys drawing, painting or sculpture would describe themselves as an artist or aspire to become a professional, they simply take pleasure from their chosen hobby and enjoy the creative process and its results. While they may have learned the basic techniques and rules of composition many years ago, they continually strive to produce better work with practice. Again, bonsai is analagous. The basic techniques of styling and training trees are relatively easily

The sinuous curves of a twin-trunked Japanese maple, Acer palmatum. *Without a sense of scale, it could be a full-sized tree: this is the art of bonsai.*

6

learned, as the rest of this book will show, and their application improves quickly with experience. For those who are already gardeners, much will be familiar, for in essence bonsai are merely potted plants, albeit those on whom more attention may be lavished than most.

Taking up bonsai as a hobby demands some commitment, since the trees you train are living plants that need regular attention, although even at the height of summer this may mean no more than five or ten minutes a day to water. It also teaches patience (since trees will only take so much pruning or shaping at one time and there are only certain times of year activities like repotting can be carried out); forward planning (for it may take several years from the initial styling before a tree begins to approach the shape and fullness originally envisaged); and, for want of a better phrase, a closer appreciation of the changing of the seasons.

In our centrally heated, artificially lit world, most of us have lost touch with the continuous turning of the year. Even keen gardeners tend to see spring as an overall event, but the bonsai enthusiast experiences the swelling of buds and emerging foliage of each species he trains individually, delights in the strong branch growth and leafy exuberance of summer, and watches for the fiery tones that colour autumn. Through winter he admires the delicate tracery of branches his work has produced in his deciduous subjects and appreciates again the stoic resistance of his evergreens, even as he worries about the effects of frosts and strong winds on their frozen rootballs.

While bonsai is quintessentially Japanese, its popularity has increased enormously over the last thirty years or so across the world. Initially at least, Japanese species were used and trees trained in traditional, and therefore Japanese, styles. Over the last ten or fifteen years, however, bonsai enthusiasts have been inspired to work with species native to their own countries and have begun to produce images of these trees in the wild. Thus in South Africa there are fine baobab bonsai, in the southern United States impressive swamp cypress, ancient olives from southern Europe and in the UK, English elms evoke in miniature the towering beauties that were lost to Dutch elm disease in the 1970s. 'Hotbeds' of new bonsai talent have sprung up in Britain, west coast America, Italy, Holland and even Russia, and it is not unheard of for trees from elsewhere to carry off some of the top prizes at Japanese bonsai shows. Specialist suppliers of tools, pots and other equipment are becoming established to service these new markets, and potters all over the world are producing exquisite bonsai containers to rival any produced in Japan.

Bonsai in Japan has also benefitted from developments elsewhere. Japan is a naturally conservative society and, like many native art forms, bonsai used to be deeply traditional. An apprentice would spend his first two years at the nursery of a bonsai master doing nothing but watering and watching his master at work. The new styles and methods developed elsewhere in the world by bonsai artists less bounded by tradition have begun to filter back, cross-fertilizing the original source.

Bonsai are also getting bigger. Some of the best trees in Europe are well over 1.5m (5ft) tall. The salient point is that the tree is a convincing image of a full-sized wild counterpart, and as such its overall size is as relatively unimportant as its actual age.

It is, therefore, an exciting time in the development of bonsai as a worldwide phenomenon. Bonsai's growing popularity means it is much easier to source tools, equipment and trees to train, and to find literature profiling quality trees. A book of this length can do little more than provide the basics of styling and training and a few good examples. It is meant to inspire you to begin this fascinating hobby, but be warned – bonsai is addictive, and many of us end up with far more trees than we originally envisaged.

Pines are perhaps the most aristocratic of bonsai, but take many years to train well.

WHAT IS BONSAI?

The literal translation of the two characters that make up the Japanese word 'bonsai' is 'to plant' (bon-) 'in a tray or pot' (-sai), but it has come to be used as both the overall term for potted, miniature trees, and a description of the processes involved in shaping and caring for them. How then did the art form originate and develop?

HISTORY

The records of early civilizations in Egypt and the Indus valley in India and China all show that growing plants in pots has a long tradition in human history. For the earliest peoples, container cultivation was based around useful plants such as food crops and medicines, however by the second millennium before the Christian era (2000BC), the Chinese were growing plants in pots simply for their aesthetic qualities – pot plants to beautify the home and/or garden. From this, it was not much of a development to begin controlling the growth patterns of such plants to display them to their best advantage. Thus began the ancient Chinese practice that is still known as 'pen-jing'.

China had a strong formative influence on the development of its near-neighbour Japan, and pen-jing seems to have been brought to Japan by some of the early buddhist monks in the ninth century, who also had a profound influence on Japanese gardening. The early years of the bonsai tradition in Japan will probably always remain obscure, and there is no single event by which a potted plant suddenly became a bonsai. Like most artistic traditions, its development was a gradual one, going through a series of trends and fashions. What is certain is that the native Japanese religion, Shinto, with its emphasis on the sanctity of nature and particular reverence for unusually shaped natural objects (both living and non-living), found in bonsai a perfect means of expression.

Although in China pen-jing trees were often combined with rocks and other plants to create landscapes in miniature, they were also trained into unusual shapes suggesting mythical creatures such as dragons, or had their trunks coiled or trained to suggest auspicious Chinese characters; there was little attempt to make them look 'natural'. No doubt early Japanese trees were similar, but by the end of the 16th century, the last part of Japan's strife-riven Muromachi period (1338-1573), naturally stunted trees were collected from the wild and kept in pots by noblemen and samurai alike, as surviving scrolls and depictions prove.

During the following Edo period (1603-1867), a peaceful time under which many native arts blossomed and developed, the idea of training collected specimens to compensate for perceived faults and give them a more natural appearance also seems to have taken hold, as did the creation of 'artificial dwarfs' from seeds and cuttings. Prints survive that show early nurseries in which several species, all in pots, were being cultivated. This is perhaps not so surprising because Japanese gardening, with its own strongly naturalistic design ethos, was also developing apace and full-sized trees were being trained into the pleasing, shapes based on those found in old trees in nature.

What made bonsai a uniquely Japanese art was its growing emphasis on such natural forms, and the copying of particular tree shapes found in the wild, almost certainly because of the influence of Shinto. By the time Japan opened her doors to foreigners after a long period of self-imposed isolation in 1868 (the beginning of the Meiji era), the techniques of producing and training bonsai were fairly well established and the hobby had become the preserve of merchants and the middle classes as much as the aristocracy. With the increased demand came a whole industry of nurseries, pot manufacturers and tool suppliers. Initially, many of these were based around Edo (modern Tokyo), but after floods and an earthquake, and with the area's growing urbanization, in 1923 many moved and settled in and around Omiya, a small town north of Tokyo on Honshu, Japan's major island. Omiya remains one of the centres of the art today.

Early European travellers to Japan at the end of the 19th century seemed nonplussed by their first encounter with bonsai, describing them as grotesquely contorted or curiously stunted, believing their creation to be some arcane and difficult Japanese art. Exhibitions were staged by Japanese nurserymen in London and Paris in the first decades of the 20th century, but bonsai never really caught on in the West until after the Second World War. American servicemen stationed in Japan after the war seem to have been instrumental in bringing trees and the art form itself home with them, but it was not until the 1950s and 1960s that books on the subject were published in English. From such small beginnings, bonsai has developed into a worldwide phenomenon, with an ever-increasing number of practitioners, and an ever-increasing list of species being tried.

Today, although it is obvious pen-jing and bonsai share a common source and similar techniques, there are still major differences in style, Japanese trees somehow looking more 'natural', Chinese ones more rugged and stylised. This is not in any way to belittle the Chinese tradition, which has its own long-established foundations.

This grey bark elm, Ulmus parvifolia, is a good example of a heavy-trunked, Chinese-style tree.

EXPLODING SOME MYTHS

Perhaps the most prevalent myth about bonsai is that it is inherently 'cruel' to its subjects, which are 'tortured' and grossly misshapen. Leaving aside whether it is possible to be 'cruel' to an organism with no pain receptors or central nervous system, if bonsai is cruel, how much crueller is it to grow an expanse of a single species crowded together and sheared to less than a centimetre tall once a week, never allowing them to flower or set seed? How many of you mow the lawn weekly in summer? If bonsai is cruel, how much crueller is it to rob a plant of its storage organs, peel them with a sharp knife then scald them in water for half an hour before enjoying a portion of boiled potatoes?

Yes, bonsai are artificially dwarfed by regular pruning and by growing them in a restricted space, the bonsai pot. They are not 'starved' of water and nutrients however – bonsai growers are generally extemely protective of their charges, having lavished a great deal of care and attention on them, watering, feeding and protecting them from the worst of winter weather, and cossetting them far more than the average houseplant.

Another myth is that because they are so small, bonsai must be special dwarf cultivars, or grown from seeds treated by some arcane oriental method to keep them tiny. In fact, they are grown from perfectly ordinary seeds or cuttings from full-sized specimens; it is regular pruning and a restricted root-run that keeps them small. Dwarf cultivars of some species are used, but their restricted growth rates make their development as bonsai a slow and sometimes painful process.

A third common myth is that bonsai are kept dwarf by regular root pruning. This is simply not the case; like any plant grown long-term in a pot, the roots of a bonsai eventually come to fill the pot, reducing its growth and making it difficult to water. Rather than simply transferring it to a larger pot, since the pot has been chosen to harmonize with the tree itself, the roots are untangled and pruned by a quarter to a third to allow the grower to replace the tree in the same pot with some fresh compost. This is done to increase or maintain the tree's vigour, not to dwarf it. The frequency of root pruning depends on the vigour of the individual tree and the size of its pot; some trees need it annually, others only every three to five years. It is branch-pruning that keeps the top of the tree small.

Bonsai need not be an expensive hobby. While good-quality, pre-trained trees can be expensive (and arguably should be, given the amount of labour and care that has gone into producing them), the materials needed to create quality trees yourself are as far away as your back garden or local garden centre. Not only is it far more satisfying to create bonsai yourself from such material, you will also learn far more about the techniques and feel a greater affinity for a tree that is 'all your own work'. It is far less discouraging to make a mistake on such a tree than on an expensive, newly purchased one. Learn the basics on nursery stock first, decide if maintaining bonsai can be fitted into your schedule (and whether you have the necessary patience), then go out and buy trees if you wish. Similarly with tools, those designed specifically for use in bonsai are still primarily imported from Japan and are usually expensive as a result, but a good set of stainless-steel tools will not magically make you a bonsai artist. Sharp pairs of scissors, secateurs and a decent set of pliers that can also cut wire are perfectly adequate to style a tree.

I have already touched on size, but it is a fairly common misconception that bonsai must be below a cerain size. There are trees only a few inches tall – in Japan these are known as 'mame' or 'bean' bonsai – but these are the exception rather than the rule. Size is unimportant providing there is a convincing impression of a full-sized tree in miniature. Bonsai can, in fact, be anything up to 2m (6ft) tall. Although most of the species commonly used are those with naturally small leaves, specimens with large leaves, such as horse chestnuts, need to be correspondingly big to be convincing.

Finally, and perhaps most importantly, bonsai are not house plants. The vast majority of so-called 'indoor bonsai' are nothing of the sort, being mass-produced, poor-quality pen-jing of tropical and sub-tropical species grown in the Far East in fields of almost pure clay. Import restrictions mean that all the soil has to be removed from their roots before they are exported to the West and replaced by sterilized growing media on arrival. If they survive this transplantation trauma, they emerge weakened

A fine display of 'mame' (miniature) bonsai staged by the Bonsai Kai Society.

into an unfamiliar growing environment. These are trees requiring tropical light levels and tropical humidities, and are not at all suited to cultivation in a dry, dark, centrally heated western home. If you must grow bonsai indoors, buy a houseplant (ideally something forgiving and tolerant like a fig or olive) and train it yourself; the result is likely to be of higher quality. There is nothing more disheartening for a beginner than to lose their first tree through no fault of their own, so stick to outdoor species that you know to be hardy in our climate – and grow them outdoors. Once you have gained experience with these, you may want to try an indoor specimen, and you will then have a better appreciation of just how low the quality of most imported stock is – but don't say I didn't warn you.

STYLES

The origin of different bonsai styles is difficult to trace, and how much the styles are a western attempt to classify the existing way trees were trained in Japan at the end of the 19th century is a moot point. Nevertheless they remain useful, particularly when the wild tree shapes they represent are borne in mind, and especially when deciding what style of tree can be created from a particular 'potensai' (potential, i.e. untrained, bonsai). Some trees can be described by more than one style as they have aspects of both, so many styles are not mutually exclusive. They should instead be regarded simply as guidelines and inspiration, not rules to which raw material must be fitted.

Some factors, derived from the characteristics of older trees, are common to nearly all the styles, however. These include, from root level upwards:

● a spread of surface roots, 'neabari', evenly distributed around the trunk (for exceptions see below) that seem to 'grip' the soil surface. 'Knee' roots, where there is a gap between root and the compost surface, should be avoided, as should roots that point straight forward towards the viewer. Surface roots are rarely found with young trees or saplings
● a solid trunk base, thickest where it joins the roots, tapering gradually to become thinner and thinner as the apex is reached. Inverse taper, where a trunk bulges to become thicker around a branch, old wound or graft is a major fault
● the thickest branch is the lowest one, with branches becoming progressively thinner and, usually, shorter higher up

the tree. Thick branches near the apex are a particularly common fault

● more than one branch emerging from the same point. The production of whorls of branches is a juvenile characteristic exhibited by many trees. Two branches placed either side of the trunk growing from the same point introduce a dominant horizontal line, stopping the eye, which is again a major fault

● crossing branches, whether crossing another branch or the trunk line itself (although there are exceptions, discussed below), and branches growing straight up, a juvenile growth pattern

● foliage growing below branches only tends to be seen on small and young trees, as the amount of shadow cast by the branches prohibits growth here in mature trees

● higher branches growing from a point directly above lower ones. This is a fault except near the apex of the tree. In nature, looking at a tree from above, its branches are usually arranged spirally around the trunk to maximize the amount of light each receives, with no large branch directly shading another

An outstanding formal upright Japanese cedar, Cryptomeria japonica, *on display at the Chelsea Flower Show 1998.*

THE MAJOR BONSAI STYLES

There are five 'classic' single-trunked bonsai styles, based on the trunk's form and angle.

Classic

Formal Upright (chokkan)

The image the formal upright is designed to conjure is of a large, majestic, mature tree growing in ideal conditions without competition from neighbours, such as in parkland. The trunk is upright, springing from a strong rootbase with thick surface roots (neabari), and tapering gradually from root level to the top of the tree with no sudden changes in thickness or swellings. The first branch should be at approximately a third of the tree's total height, with subsequent branches spirally arranged up the trunk, getting closer together in a regular pattern towards the apex, and progressively thinner and shorter. Formal upright trees have an overall triangular shape with the apex directly above the root flare, or above and slightly forward of it so the tree seems to 'bow' toward the viewer (a common visual 'trick' in many styles to increase the tree's apparent depth).

Depending on the sources consulted, branch arrangement in this style can be quite exact; the pattern should always be left, back, right – or right, back, left – in sequence up the trunk and the distance between tiers of branches should reduce consecutively with mathematical precision. The branches are invariably trained into the same overall shape and profile to help unify the design, either horizontally, below horizontal to weep slightly, or horizontal with a slightly concave profile so they seem to 'cup' their foliage. The part of the branch nearest the trunk is kept clear of foliage, since leaves close to the trunk is a juvenile characteristic, and looking down from above, each branch holds a triangle, lozenge or pear shape of foliage. All leaves growing from the underside of the branch are removed since, this is a juvenile characteristic and spoils the line of the branches. The foliage pads or 'clouds' in any bonsai, but particularly with formal upright, need to be separated from the next branch up by a clear space, or a 'negative area', like the main branches of a mature tree. This is one of the most important 'visual tricks' in bonsai that convinces the viewer they are looking at a old tree rather than an amorphous blob of foliage. The trunks of formal uprights are unobstructed by foliage for at least two-thirds of its height, but after this it is acceptable to allow foliage from the side branches to grow in front of it to add visual interest as the apex is approached.

A 'worm's eye' view of the underside of a branch of the Scots pine shown below right, showing the underlines cleared of foliage as in a mature tree.

The maidenhair tree, Ginkgo biloba, *is often trained into an traditional upright 'candle flame' shape.*

Clearly, to train a tree to such an exacting standard requires not only time and patience, but the selection of unusual and rare potensai with near-perfect branch structure. Pines, spruces, firs, *Cryptomeria japonica*, junipers and more unusual subjects like dawn redwoods (*Metasequoia glyptostroboides*) and swamp cypress (*Taxodium distichum*), and other species that commonly adopt pyramid shapes in nature, are most suited to formal upright style. Unless a potensai is screaming out to be used as a formal upright this is not a style recommended for beginners, as not only is it fairly restricted in terms of training, but it can also take several years for formal upright bonsai to begin to look good.

Informal Upright (moyogai)

Something of an all-embracing style, informal upright describes a multitude of bonsai that do not fit into the other categories, and represents the growth pattern of an 'average', asymmetrical, mature tree. Although it still needs to exhibit good taper from root to apex, the trunks of informal upright trees may

have several curves, a single major curve or a definite change of direction in the trunk line. The branches are arranged much more loosely around the trunk, so that although the overall shape often remains broadly triangular, it may not be a symmetrical triangle and the apex of the tree is not always directly above the rootbase.

A powerful informal upright dwarf Scots pine, Pinus sylvestris 'Beuvronensis', with driftwood.

In designs with curves to the trunk, branches are placed on the outside of the curves, not inside since this is unnatural. As with the formal upright, the lowest branches are the heaviest and most widely-spaced, the thickness and distance between them reducing as the apex is approached. Although branches are distributed to left, right and back in most designs, the sequence is not so rigidly followed as in the formal upright. Providing they do not overlap each other when viewed from above and that the whole forms a pleasing, balanced image, it is quite acceptable to have two left or two right branches in the sequence. Like the formal upright, the negative areas between the foliage pads are just as important to the definition of the tree's design as the foliage itself. Shaping the branches so they have a similar profile when observed from the side, whether horizontal, downward-pointing, concave or even convex – rising slightly away from the trunk and descending at the tip – again helps bring the overall design together. Towards the apex, foliage can grow in front of the trunk and it is even possible to

Left: A white pine (Pinus parviflora) *with the heavy lower trunk that often characterizes a graft onto more vigorous black pine* (Pinus thunbergii) *rootstock.*

Right: An outstanding red hawthorn, Crataegus laevigata *'Paul's Scarlet'.*

have thin upper branches crossing the main trunk line, although none should project directly forward.

Being such an all-embracing style, almost all species are suited to informal upright, deciduous, coniferous and flowering trees alike and, given its relative freedom, it is perhaps the best style for the beginner – unless the characteristics of a particular potensai suggest otherwise.

Slanting style mountain pine (Pinus mugo) with the great sense of movement typical of the style.

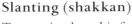

Slanting (shakkan)

Trees trained to this format seem rare in the West. Essentially a sub-set of the informal upright style, shakkan trees may have curved or straight trunks that lean at a definite, relatively constant angle, often around 45 degrees. The overall impression is of a tree that has been forced by adverse environmental conditions, whether wind or lack of light, to grow away from its preferred, near-vertical form. To be convincing, the surface roots on the side opposite the lean should be particularly well-developed, giving the impression they are holding the tree against the forces of gravity, and the first branch should appear a third of the way up the trunk on the side opposite the lean. This helps to visually balance the tree. Similar rules for branch distribution to informal upright are followed, with the ideal being tiers in groups of three.

Branches should be horizontal or slightly downward-pointing, the latter giving a good contrast with the trunk angle. Those growing away from the slant are usually longer than those opposite, since in nature branches on this side would get more light. A common visual trick is to have the branches on the open side rise slightly at the junction with the trunk then sweep out and down, and those on the inner side fall slightly at the junction then sweep out. The foliage on slanting style trees forms roughly horizontal or slightly domed masses and, except for the apex, is usually fuller on the open side. Slanting style, conjuring up as it does trees subjected to the ravages of wind and weather, is best suited to rugged coniferous subjects such as pines, junipers and larches; deciduous trees in the style are relatively rare. It is, however, well-suited to potensai with a natural lean or with roots concentrated on one side of the trunk and, when well-executed, produces dynamic trees with a real sense of movement.

Semi-cascade (han-kengai) and Cascade (kengai) styles

Since these styles are so similar, they will be treated together. Semi-cascade trees are trained almost horizontally, with the apex at or just below the rim of the pot, whereas the trunks of full cascade trees plunge well below the rim and often even the base of the pot. Both are dramatic styles and are intended to represent trees growing high on a cliff-face, shaped by exposure to wind, snow and landslides to grow out and down in search of light and shelter. As with slanting style, in nature the force of gravity would exert strong pulling forces on the roots on the opposite side to the main trunk, so a marked bulge of roots would form there.

Although a semi-cascade is essentially always viewed from one side, branch placement follows the same pattern as in more upright styles, that is to the right, left or behind the main trunk line. In practice this means branches are distributed above, below and behind the trunk, but unlike in other styles the main thrust of the branches usually follows the line of the trunk to the side. Thus branches above ascend at an angle and then tend towards horizontal, while those below, which are usually fewer in number and concentrated more towards the apex, descend first then are trained sideways. Looking from the apex back along the trunk line, the overall structure should be similar to looking at a formal or informal upright from above.

Semi-cascades can appear two-dimensional, so the trunk is often given fairly abrupt curves and changes in direction both up and down and towards and away from the viewer, with the main branches placed at the outsides of the curves. Although the apex is actually the tip of the main trunk, a second apex is often created above the main trunk line close to the pot. A side branch

A fine semi-cascade style crabapple, Malus x micromalus. *This hybrid is notable for its tiny fruit, making it ideal for bonsai.*

from here, trained over the main trunk curve opposite the cascade branch, helps to counterbalance and stabilize the design. The apex near the rootball, usually formed from the first major branch, can easily become more vigorous than the apex at the end of the trunk, so the grower needs to be aware of this and keep the pot apex pruned more closely than the true apex to equalize their vigour. As in other styles, foliage on the undersides of the branches suggests immaturity and is removed. The foliage pads in semi-cascade are often relatively small and sparse to concentrate attention on the fluid lines of the trunk, nearly always extending furthest in the main direction of growth.

Many genera are suitable for the semi-cascade style, although those that are flexible species such as junipers and pines are easiest to shape, particularly if they have a marked curve near the rootball and existing horizontal growth, or a strong, heavy first branch on an otherwise upright tree that can form the main trunk if the existing trunk is removed. Conifers are well-suited to the style and probably most commonly seen, although flowering and fruiting types such as cotoneaster or deciduous genera such as hornbeam and beech can be equally striking.

Full cascade bonsai are relatively rare but are one of the most striking styles to create and display, symbolizing as they do a tree clinging tenaciously to life under the most adverse conditions. Unlike in a semi-cascade where the 'front' of the tree is in fact its side, a full cascade plunges over the lip of the pot and is trained down well below this, and often beyond its base too, with foliage pads to right and left. Traditional cascade pots are tall and narrow to accommodate this form. A distinction is sometimes made between cascades with a straight trunk (formal) and those with curves (informal cascades). Informal cascades are easier to 'balance' as the main branches can spring from the outsides of the curves, whereas formal cascades are, in essence, formal upright trees with a major bend to them, their branches conforming to the same triadic arrangement turned through 180 degrees. As with semi-cascades, the other major design choice is whether the trunk should exhibit a naked curve down into the style, or if it should be topped with a secondary apex. Again, it is easier to balance the design with this second apex but the tendency for the true apex, down at the bottom of a full cascade, to lose vigour is even more marked. The tree's natural tendency is to grow upwards towards the light, so it will concentrate vigour in those branches with the highest foliage, bypassing those on the cascade branch itself. Pruning must be tailored to counteract this tendency therefore, with growth on the sub-apex clipped back hard and that on the lower apex given almost free rein.

Cascade is perhaps one of the most artificial of styles and one of the most difficult to achieve convincing results in, and therefore not recommended for complete beginners. Aside from the vigour problems, tall traditional pots are inherently unstable and may need securing to the bonsai shelves. Their very depth makes them difficult to water – the top may dry out while the lower part of the pot remains sodden. Like semi-cascade, this is a style probably more common in Chinese pen-jing than in bonsai.

The other styles are either variations on these five 'classics', or they have more than one trunk stemming from the same root system, are group plantings involving more than one tree to create a miniature woodland, or they involve rocks of a greater or lesser size.

Windswept (fukinagashi)

Trees in the windswept style conjure up the image of trees growing in extremely exposed situations like cliff tops or on the coast, where a strong prevailing wind comes from a single direction. The windward side of the trunk remains almost clear of branches, or with what branches there are dead or almost shorn of foliage. Almost all these branches should be concentrated on the leeward side. The trunks of such trees often lean away from the wind, making the style best suited to those that would otherwise be trained as slanting, or semi-cascade, but windswept style is also an excellent way of using potensai that have an extremely one-sided branch development. Despite their strong form, windswept trees are nevertheless quite difficult to balance and make look convincing. This is one of the few styles where it is acceptable to have a major branch crossing in front of the trunk if the 'prevailing wind' would have made it grow in that direction. Most species are suitable.

Driftwood (sharimiki)

This is one of the most popular styles in the West and involves areas of dead, bleached wood on a tree's trunk (shari) and dead branches (jins). Evocative of ancient trees, particularly those growing in exposed conditions, it probably arose early in bonsai's history when old, naturally dwarfed trees were collected from the mountains. Whether as a result of exposure to strong winds, physical injury, decay or animal browsing, such specimens often displayed areas of dead, bleached wood symbolic of age and stoicism in the face of adversity. The techniques for artificially creating such

The jins and shari of the Scots pine shown on p. 19.

Heavy trunked driftwood style needle juniper, Juniperus rigida.

'injuries' are now well established, involving stripping areas of a tree's bark and carving its wood, in large specimens even with powertools, before preserving it with a mixture of lime and sulphur. Although undoubtedly dramatic, the style has perhaps been overused, particularly in recent years. Coniferous trees such as pines, junipers and cedars are most commonly used, as these have resinous wood that resists decay and tends to persist on the tree. Only a few species of deciduous trees, such as olives and oaks, tend to hold on to their deadwood in this manner. Trees with driftwood can be trained in most other styles, with informal upright being the most common. Converting branch stubs into jins following pruning is a commonly used disguise to avoid a major scar on the trunk and tends to make a tree of any style look older.

Literati style cedar, Cedrus brevifolia, a species endemic to Cyprus. The unusual bulge of roots at left helps balance the dynamic thrust of the trunk to the right.

Literati

There is no direct translation of the word 'literati' which is a term from China that describes an educated class of scholars and artists and is also a label for their 'South China School' of landscape painting. This school was characterised by a large preponderance of mountain landscapes and tall, curiously contorted trees depicted with relatively few brush-strokes. Literati-style bonsai are often similarly simple looking. The best natural model is perhaps our own Scots pine, which forms a tall, sparsely branched and often flat-topped profile in maturity. Literati bonsai are usually tall, though well-tapered, often exhibiting sharp curves and changes of direction in their trunk line, with only a few branches occuring towards the top of the tree and relatively small foliage pads. The relationship between these and the negative areas of the crown are particularly important, as an amorphous 'mop-head' of foliage is a sign of juvenility. In fact the style's simplicity is deceptive, since balancing the image with so few branches and foliage pads is much more difficult than it looks. Nevertheless, literati is one of the most elegant of bonsai styles, the curves in the trunk symbolizing the difficulties the tree has faced in its life, and the sparse branching analogous to the minimalist simplicity beloved of the Zen Buddhist monks who largely created it. The genus most often chosen for literati bonsai is the quintessential tree of the mountains, the pine. Scots pine (*Pinus sylvestris*) has proved itself as good if not better suited than the traditional Japanese species, black pine (*Pinus thunbergii*) and white pine (*Pinus parviflora*). Other coniferous genera such as larch and juniper can also be used, but the style is less suited to deciduous trees, unless they are old, rugged-looking and relatively slender specimens.

*A group planting of Japanese larch (*Larix kaempferi*) on an artificial ceramic slab with a rugged feel.*

Trees with rocks

There are three different styles that make use of a combination of trees and rocks; planting trees on, in or over carefully selected stones.

Slab planting

Here, a large, usually flat, rock takes the place of the bonsai pot, with the tree or trees planted into a mound of potting medium formed on it. If the rock is relatively flat, this is usually held in place by a low 'wall' of clay, with the whole covered in mosses or other small groundcover plants to stabilize the surface. Once the two have been united, the tree's feeder roots will grow down into the rock, and beyond scraping away the compost surface and replacing it with a little fresh material, rock-planted bonsai are not usually repotted.

Well-executed, slab plantings look extremely natural and it is even possible to produce artificial slabs in pottery, or using chicken wire covered in fibreglass and car filler-paste, painted in appropriately muted tones.

Clinging to rock (ishitsuki)

In this style a rock with a natural crevice is chosen, or a planting hole is carved out of a soft rock such as tufa, and a tree planted into it. The plant is usually a small one, to give the impression of a tree clinging to life on the ledge of a much larger cliff. The whole bonsai is often displayed in a shallow dish of water both to keep the planting more moist and to suggest an island (the 'Isles of the Blessed' being a common motif in both Chinese and Japanese mythology). It is important that the rock complements the tree and has a rough, complex surface, and that the tree is trained to harmonize with the rock, for example cascading down the 'cliff face'. This is one of the few areas of bonsai where dwarf cultivars are extensively employed; it is important that the scale of the tree does not exceed that of the rock, so extremely slow growth rates are a positive advantage. As with slab planting, ishitsuki trees are not repotted.

The contrast between the light roots and dark rock, purpling autumn foliage and red berries make this Cotoneaster horizontalis a beautiful composition.

Root over rock (sekijoju)

One of the most dramatic and evocative of bonsai styles. In root over rock trees thick surface roots flow down the crevices and cracks of a rock that the tree seems melded to, before plunging into the surface of the compost. The style evokes trees clinging to life in an area subject to severe soil erosion such as a riverbank or steep mountainside. Root over

rock is a favourite among beginners to bonsai because it is so dramatic, and producing a convincing effect is neither as time consuming or difficult as it is often made out (see p.46). The rock should be hard and inert, such as granite or dolomite that will not crumble with time in the way tufa would, for example. Ideally, it should also have vertical cracks and crevices and a horizontal 'saddle' for the tree to sit on. Unlike ishitsuki, sekijoju trees are often much larger than the rock, although again the design of the trunk and branches should be carefully matched to the stone, and the colour of the rock should not clash with the tree's bark or leaves. The most common types for root over rock are the Japanese trident maple (*Acer buergerianum*) and various species of fig (*Ficus*), all of which produce thick, fleshy roots. Many other genera such as yew,

juniper, pyracantha and even ivy are suitable, however, with the rugged nature of the resulting image making it well-suited to conifers. Root over rock bonsai are repotted as a unit in the normal way, with the rock effectively becoming part of the trunk of the specimen.

Multiple trunks

Although bonsai with more than one trunk are not as common as those with a single trunk, there are several well-established methods of producing trees with more than a single trunk. Two or three trunks emerging near the root crown are preferred, but co-dominant trunks of similar size and thickness are best

An exquisitely balanced twin trunk Japanese maple (Acer palmatum).

avoided. If one trunk emerges much above soil level, it will look more like a badly formed first branch than another trunk. With three trunk specimens, the smallest should be the one in the middle to avoid an artificial 'graded' appearance. In training, other than the first branch being placed on the most subordinate trunk, which helps unify the design, the branches

of both or all three trunks are treated as a single unit and trained accordingly. If a suitable potensai cannot be found for a twin or triple trunk, coppicing a suitable plant down to near ground level should result in a multitude of shoots being thrown up, the best two or three of which can be retained and grown on. Alternatively, two or three saplings can be root-pruned and planted closely together so that as they grow the trunks unite.

A group planting of Zelkova serrata. The variable autumn colours indicates it was assembled from seedlings.

Because individuals vary in factors such as shoot emergence, autumn colour and timing of leaf fall (above), with any multiple tree planting it is preferable that cuttings from the same plant are rooted and used, rather than trees raised from seed. Traditionally, other than twin-trunk or two tree plantings, only an odd number of trees or trunks are used in multiple plantings. This partly reflects an ancient oriental belief that even numbers are inherently more unlucky than odd ones, but particularly with plantings of less than eleven, it is much more difficult to achieve a convincingly assymetrical look with an even number of trees. Odd numbers from three to nine simply look more natural.

Another way of achieving several trunks with the same characteristics is to use a single tree, but plant it on its side and train each branch as an individual trunk. This is known as a raft bonsai or 'idakabuki', and is another way of making use of one-sided potensai. Initially, branches on the opposite side are

Style development

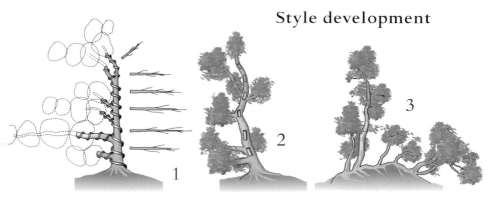

removed (1), then the bark opposite each branch is wounded and hormone rooting powder applied (2), then the trunk is half buried in a large training pot and the branches wired upwards. Eventually the new roots will be strong enough to allow the original rootball to be cut off (3). The original trunk can be planted straight across the pot, but more depth will be introduced by forming curves so that the trunks appear distributed from front to back.

Forest plantings

Groups of several individual trees can also be used in bonsai to create the image of more substantial groves or sections of woodland. An odd number should be chosen (see above) with trunks of varying heights and thicknesses. One major advantage of this style of bonsai is that it is quite easy to form a convincingly old image relatively quickly, and inexpensive

A well balanced group planting of Japanese beech, Fagus crenata.

Trees from group plantings

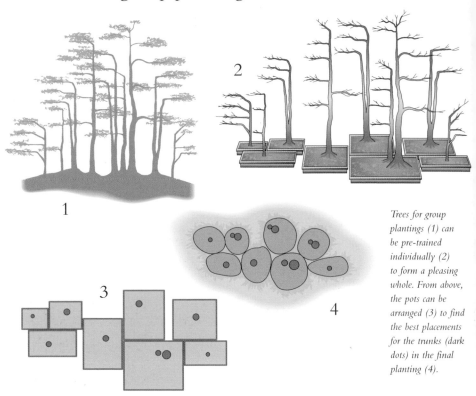

1

2

3

4

Trees for group plantings (1) can be pre-trained individually (2) to form a pleasing whole. From above, the pots can be arranged (3) to find the best placements for the trunks (dark dots) in the final planting (4).

young seedlings or saplings can be used that do not cost much or require much training. Trees that have grown in a forest environment have to compete for light and are usually therefore relatively tall and thin and, unlike other forms of bonsai, ascending branches reaching up as if in search of light are quite acceptable in group plantings.

In order to increase the apparent depth of the planting, the largest tree is almost always set at the front of the pot (or slab, since mini-forests on slabs can look most effective and are usually cheaper than a large bonsai pot), with the smallest and thinnest at the back. Since trees that are far away from the viewer always look smaller because of perspective, this visual trick makes the planting seem much deeper. The usual method of training a small group is to have the largest tree a third to a half of the way along the pot (never in the middle) with the

A literati style group planting of Japanese larch, Larix kaempferi, *with the sparse, airy feel typical of the style.*

others arranged asymetrically, with varying distances between the trunks on either side. The heights of the trees grades down from the main tree, and the trunks of the outer trees may lean slightly away from the vertical as if in search of more light. The foliage of the whole planting should form a broadly triangular outline from the crown of the largest tree downwards. Trees with one-sided branching are ideally suited to forest plantings, for use either side of the main tree.

With larger plantings, a main group of trees can be separated from a sub-group and formed into a smaller triangle some distance away. Ideally, each trunk should emerge from a slight mound of soil suggesting the buttress of roots below and again increasing the apparent perspective. Piecing together a forest planting is largely a matter of trial and error, examining each tree in relation to the main one until the most pleasing and asymmetrical arrangement is found. For those who prefer uniformity, it would be best to raise a forest of cuttings from the same source with the same characteristics. However this would not be found in nature, where each forest tree is an individual.

Deciding on a style

From the above discussion, it should be obvious that although some potensai were almost made for a particular style, others could prove well-suited to several. Bear in mind that there is no 'right' or 'wrong' way to style a bonsai and that different growers given the same raw material may well produce very differently styled trees. Likewise, perfect examples of raw material are extremely few and far between, and initial styling often involves compromises from the ideal. The rules are there to be used – and bent where necessary – not slavishy followed. To do so would be to attempt to create idealized trees, forced into forms to which they may not be suited. Always remember that bonsai involves living things, each of which has its own natural form and characteristics. At its best, bonsai is about liberating an image that a tree has already formed within itself, or guiding it into its most satisfactory shape. Don't push too far to try and turn a tree into something that is not, at least partly, already there.

Remember that the techniques involved in styling and shaping bonsai are skills like any other – your first attempts may be awkward and not amount to much, but you are at the bottom of a steep learning curve. As pruning and wiring become second nature and your experience in selecting and shaping trees advances, your skills will improve and your trees with them. Providing you have not killed them with impatience (which can easily be done), the worst that can happen is they will never make a good bonsai. I keep one of my first attempts, a horse chestnut whose large leaves and thick, coarse branches are not really suited to bonsai, as a reminder that we all had to start somewhere. My first Japanese maple 'bonsai' is now taller than I am and rapidly becoming a full-sized garden tree – although I have not yet discounted the possibility of cutting it back drastically and lifting it for a second styling. Planting failed trees out in the garden and allowing them to 'bulk up' for the future is one way of dealing with poor specimens, as well as a good way of quickly thickening up potensai that lack obvious styling options.

An extremely powerful looking black pine, Pinus thunbergii. *The stout trunk and heavy lowest branch were produced by several years growing in the ground.*

Sources of supply

There are two main groups of bonsai growers, those who have the means to buy themselves a collection and teach themselves how to maintain it, and those who develop their own trees from 'raw materials'. While some of the former group may consider themselves to be connoisseurs, and are highly critical when choosing a tree and skilled at watering, repotting and clipping their charges to their pre-existing shapes, I would argue they cannot be considered bonsai artists, since they have created nothing. The only way to learn bonsai as an art form is to practise all stages, and in particular the initial choice and styling of trees from potensai. You will not only gain a better insight into the training techniques and their application, you will forge stronger bonds with your subjects having shaped them yourself. Of course, there is no way one person can train a tree more than a century old and you may decide large, specimen bonsai are your ultimate aim, but by learning the basics of training on trees you have selected yourself, you will gain the experience and skills necessary to take on the care of old and expensive subjects, and actually be able to improve their shapes, rather than merely maintain them.

Given these provisos, where can the budding bonsai enthusiast find suitable trees to train?

Collecting from the wild

The oldest and most venerable bonsai in Japan are almost without exception trees that exposed, adverse conditions made into natural dwarfs in the wild, usually in the mountains.

An unconventional zelkova bonsai best described as 'clump style', created from a larger tree regularly cut back hard or coppiced. The natural looking hollowed wounds are known as 'uros'.

Elsewhere in Europe, experienced bonsai growers are beginning to seek out similar material from areas such as the Alps and Italian Appenines. Collecting from the wild, however, is not easy and cannot be recommended for beginners, as collected material invariably loses much of its root system, requires specialist aftercare and may take several years to recover enough to go through even basic training. Older collected material is often much less vigorous than younger plants and, despite its existing aged appearance and relatively large size, can take many years to assume the required form.

Aside from the practical difficulties of finding suitable wild material, there is an important ethical point to consider. Bonsai growers are often drawn to the hobby by an affinity for nature, and even if not pre-existing, working with living trees and seeing their response to the changing seasons usually makes them more aware of the wider natural environment, its trees in particular, and the need to protect and conserve wild areas. Whether you can justify taking a wild plant out of its natural environment is very much a personal decision, but technically it is illegal under the Wildlife and Countryside Act to uproot any wild plant in Britain. There are also protected areas such as National Parks (and their Scottish equivalents) which, although ideal hunting grounds for stunted material, are protected exactly because of their wild plants. Collecting from such areas should not take place under any circumstances.

My personal view is that my own collecting from the 'wild' is limited to already degraded or disturbed ground such as quarries and waste ground, areas that are due for development and about to be cleared of vegetation, or areas that are being positively managed for wildlife. Voluntary work with a local wildlife trust often involves scrub clearance – for example, promoting meadowland provided me with a compact hazel that has made a fine bonsai, and preventing trees establishing on the surface of a raised bog in Scotland produced several young birches. Both of these areas were actually nature reserves, but in removing native scrubland pioneer species like birch, hawthorn and hazel, their wildlife value was actually being enhanced, and I was in a sense actually 'rescuing' trees that would otherwise have been discarded.

Hedges that have fallen into disuse or been replaced by fencing due to gappiness can be a great source as they have been regularly cut back to keep them compact. Keep your eye out in your local area and collecting sites will become obvious. One point that should always be stressed is that, legally speaking, you must obtain the permission of the landowner to lift the material (the reponse is usually a bemused 'yes' in my experience).

Unwanted garden shrubs

Most gardens, however small, have trees and shrubs that were either planted in the wrong place or have grown bigger than originally envisaged, and some of these can make excellent potensai. Not only are they free, but collecting such plants gives valuable experience in how to lift more mature material from elsewhere, establish it in a container and begin shaping it. Such common shrubs as cotoneasters, azaleas, ivies, berberis and especially 'dwarf' conifers, that have proved anything but dwarf when mature, can all make fine bonsai relatively quickly.

Some species of pine can grow up to 80m (90 yd) tall, yet lend themselves very well to the exacting art of bonsai.

In selecting suitable material, concentrate on an interesting trunk line and, ideally, good surface roots rather than a good pattern of branches. A suitable branching pattern can be developed around an interesting trunk, but a poor, untapered trunk line cannot be improved on, no matter how good the branches. Don't be afraid to chop material back to a fraction of its original height, and consider using an existing low branch as replacement for a poorly-tapered or badly shaped trunk.

Cutting collected material back hard, whether from the wild or a garden, is in fact a prudent way to improve its survival. Invariably, a lot of the plants' roots will have been left in the ground and those that remain are unlikely to be able to supply all of the existing branches. Removing superfluous thick branches near the apex, and cutting back hard the long, whippy ones that remain, reduces the demands on the damaged root system and makes survival much more likely. Even if you do not have a clear idea of the style the collected material is going to be trained to, it is usually obvious which areas can be discarded. If you envisage a style with deadwood or jins, leave a fairly lengthy stub but remove the foliage.

The method of lifting potensai from the garden or wild is the same. The ideal time, particularly for deciduous species, is mid-autumn, after leaf fall but while the weather is still warm enough to allow some root growth. Early spring, just as the buds begin to swell, is the next best time. These timings also hold true for conifers and evergreens, since their growth is also at its minimum. Lifting trees in late spring or summer when they are in full growth is asking for trouble as is collecting in winter, when not only is the ground likely to be hard, but frost can severely damage any open wounds.

The first step in preparing to lift material is to find a suitable container. Relatively large flower pots, wooden boxes or even old washing up bowls with holes bored through the base are all fine, since the important thing is to re-establish the tree in a suitable growing medium, not to display it at this stage (for compost recipes, see Maintenance and Refinement, p. 70). Depending on the size of the specimen, dig a circular trench with a trowel or spade at least 20-30cm (8-12in) out from the trunk, depending on the size of the tree. Any thick roots that are encountered should be cut cleanly with a pair of secateurs. With garden stock, you can lessen the chance of failure by undercutting the plant about 30cm (12in) down, and filling the trench with a free-draining mixture of compost and sand or gravel. Do this in spring, and the potensai should have filled the trench with new, fibrous roots by autumn or the following spring, when it can be lifted with a much greater chance of success.

Cut back the branches to compensate for the root damage. It is usually easier to decide on which branches to remove once the tree is out of the ground, however, so when the taproots have been severed (a spade with a sharpened edge can be useful here, as can the leverage of a garden fork), lift the whole rootball and scrape away the upper part to reveal the surface roots. So long as the tree is dormant, take time to decide on the best trunk line for the front, and prune off unwanted branches either close to the trunk, or leave stubs for jins.

Bonsai growers are as divided as arborists over whether to use wound sealant, some arguing its application merely seals in fungal spores in an ideal environment, while others say it keeps them out and prevents the tree losing much needed moisture. With the sorts of large wounds that are often formed on collected material, wound sealant may be wise, but stick to a rubber-based formulation from a specialist bonsai dealer rather than a tar-based type such as Arbrex, which will permanently stain the bark. An effective alternative is a kind of sticky green plasticine used in flower arranging to secure material into vases.

Once superfluous branches have been removed, the rootball can be reduced. Carefully tease out as much of the rootball as possible, cutting back any long, thick roots and sealing their ends if necessary. If the soil the tree was growing in was heavy and full of clay, try to remove as much of it as possible without damaging the important fibrous 'feeder' roots, as a mass of heavy soil around the inner rootball can rot the base of the trunk in a well-watered pot. Otherwise leave some of the original soil closest to the trunk. Place a layer of free-draining compost in the base of the selected container and sit the tree in it, spreading the roots out as evenly as possible around the trunk. Fill up with compost around the sides and work it in well with fingers or a blunt stick to avoid air pockets. Even if the tree seems reasonably stable in the pot, it is as well to either wire in the rootball to the base of the pot or tie the trunk to the edges of the pot with at least three ties to ensure it cannot rock in the wind. This takes the place of staking a tree in the ground until it is established and stops fragile new roots from snapping below ground. Whatever the weather, water in the tree well to ensure good contact between roots and compost. If the tree was lifted in the autumn, protect it from the worst winter weather by placing in a cold greenhouse or unheated shed, and keep it out of drying winds.

The timing of the first styling depends on how the tree reacts to the following spring. If it shoots normally and grows away strongly, it may be ready for initial styling by late summer, however if it shoots late or weakly and exhibits any dieback, allow it to grow unhindered for at least a year, preferably two. The wait will be worth it, as with restored vigour it will respond much more quickly to training.

Container-grown plants

By far the most convenient and widest range of potensai can usually be had from your local garden centre. Because such material has been grown all its life in a pot, it can be styled immediately and potted into a bonsai dish relatively quickly; there is no waiting for the correct season to lift and the inevitable loss of vigour. There is usually a range of material of each species or cultivar to choose from and you can pick those best suited to particular styles. Invariably there is a much wider range of species from all over the world to select from than could be had from the wild or from a garden. Often, plants that have not grown well or are small and misshapen from a gardener's point of view make good bonsai, and these can sometimes be picked up at a reduced price. Small specialist nurseries can be even cheaper, though their selection may not be so wide. Some of the best bonsai in the country began life in a garden centre or specialist nursery, and most of my own collection has been developed from such trees. Some specialist bonsai nurseries, as well as selling trained bonsai, also sell much cheaper field- or container-grown 'starter material'. These are an excellent choice for the beginner as they tend to be fairly large, have had a modicum of initial training so usually have good taper and branch structure, and are established in their pots so training can begin immediately.

The factors to look for when selecting container-grown stock include a strong trunk line with good taper, or a suitably

A group of small bonsai all less than 30cm tall. Left to right: Chamaecyparis obtusa 'Pygmea', Acer palmatum 'Shishigashira', Zelkova serrata and Pinus aristata, bristlecone pine, one of the longest-lived trees in the world.

placed side-branch that can be trained up into a replacement leader; heavy lower branches (for most styles); not too many thick upper branches, or ones placed towards the envisaged back of the tree that can be pruned away without leaving visible scars; compact foliage with relatively short internodes (the distance between individual leaves); and reasonably well-distributed roots. This last point can be difficult to ascertain as container-grown plants are invariably potted too deep so that no roots are generally visible. The solution is to scrape away the compost around the trunk of a promising specimen until you begin to reach the first roots, which should at least allow you to see if the root system is completely one-sided or worse, girdles the trunk. When selecting coniferous subjects, steer clear of dwarf or slow-growing selections, which will take an age to develop, unless you are planning a small-scale rock planting or group. With subjects that are difficult to strike from cuttings like pines, cedars and named selections of Japanese maples that are invariably grafted, pay particular attention to the area of the graft. Bad grafts produce an unsightly swelling and, therefore, inverse taper, that will always be obvious on the trunk and are a major fault. Good grafts are less obvious, and may become almost invisible with time, but ungrafted individuals raised from seed nearly always make better bonsai, if available.

It is also possible to get part of an existing plant, whether growing in a pot or in the ground, to form roots by a process known as 'air layering'. Quite substantial branches that will produce nice chunky trees can be successfully rooted by this method, which is best done in spring just as the buds begin to swell, and given a degree of formative pruning while still attached.

Choose a suitably well-tapered and interesting branch (just below a fork is good for producing twin-trunked material) and decide exactly where you want the roots to begin to form. Either completely ring the branch below this by removing a strip of bark 2-3cm ($\frac{3}{4}$-1$\frac{1}{4}$ in) wide right around it (quicker, but more risky) or leave one or two thin strips of bark undamaged to continue supplying the branch (safer, but slower). Apply a little hormone rooting powder to the wounded area, then either wrap it with a thick layer of spagnum moss, keeping it in place with a layer of polythene tied above and below the wound, or cut open a flower pot so you can wrap it around the branch, secure it with wire, and fill with an open, gritty compost mixture. The moss method will stay moist, but the pot method will require periodic watering. After several months, unwrap to check for rooting. The vigour, or lack of it, of the branch above the layer is the best guide. Usually, enough roots will have formed by the end of the growing season for the layer to be carefully severed from its parent. The moss must be carefully teased away from the new roots before potting up the layer if this method was used, whereas layers rooted in a pot have the advantage that the roots are already growing in compost. Pot into a large training pot in the usual way (see p. 41), making sure the plant is held firmly in its pot by ties or wires, as the new roots are fragile and prone to breaking if the layer rocks about. Keep it in a sheltered, shady spot and protect from low temperatures until it is growing away well, usually the following spring.

Species for beginners

Good trees for beginners (see list p. 89) are those with strong powers of recuperation and an unfussy nature as to soil type and water requirements, those that will bud-back strongly on to older wood; those that have flexible wood that is easy to wire

An outstanding red leaved Japanese maple, Acer palmatum 'Deshojo', created from an air-layer of a larger tree.

and shape; those that have relatively small foliage; branches that will thicken up relatively quickly; and are fully hardy in the UK. Some of the best deciduous sorts that fit this bill are cotoneaster species such as *C. horizontalis*, trident maple (although these may need winter protection in colder areas), field maple, hawthorn, birches, larches (coniferous, but decidous), crabapples, small-leaved cherries and willows (easy to root from substantial cuttings). The list does not include Japanese maples, which, despite their beauty, can be touchy as regards potting, watering and placement and are usually grafted. Wait until you have gained more experience with easier subjects and can assess grafted specimens better. The trident maple is similar and probably a better choice for novices, but may require winter protection. Good broad-leaved evergreens for beginners include evergreen cotoneaster species, pyracantha, box and ivies.

Perhaps the best conifers for new enthusiasts are junipers (virtually all species and cultivars, particularly those with scale-like rather than needle-like foliage), yews and false cypress (*Chamaecyparis*). Pines (many species with relatively short needles), spruces (*Picea*), cedars (*Cedrus*) and firs (*Abies*) are not difficult, but their single growth spurt a year means they have their own pruning needs and producing a convincing bonsai may take several years of training. Dawn redwood and swamp cypress are two relatively new species to bonsai that are both deciduous conifers with good autumn colour and the flexibility to be a delight to train, but both require winter protection and are not that easy to find.

TRAINING METHODS

From our existing sources, it would seem that during the early days of pen-jing and bonsai, trees were almost always collected from the wild and pruned only roughly to shape, leaving their natural forms largely untouched. At some point in China, however, a grower hit on the idea that these natural shapes could actually be improved by selective pruning, and pen-jing as an art form was born. Varying styles developed in different areas of China, with trees ultimately being specially raised rather than collected. The Chinese taste for dramatic images led to bold, heavy trunks and branches with jagged outlines and abrupt changes in direction. Once bonsai began taking its own path in Japan, trees with more naturalistic characters evolved, and these differences still exist today. The single biggest difference between the training methods used in pen-jing and bonsai is that the Chinese trees tend to be produced by a method known as 'clip and grow', essentially allowing shoots or whole branches to grow long and thicken, then pruning them back hard to a bud that will grow in another direction. Chunky trees with thick trunks and angular branches tend to result from this. More often than not, aside from an initial hard pruning to establish the basic shape, Japanese bonsai have been largely formed by wiring, often of every single branch and twig. Both methods have their uses and drawbacks and are by no means mutually exclusive.

This impressive hornbeam (Carpinus betulus) shows the story of its 'clip and grow' training. The well-healed wound at centre and second 'chop' to the trunk higher up, obscured by foliage, show where the original leaders were cut back to thinner side branches. The abrupt 'steps' in the taper will reduce over time.

STYLING A CONTAINERIZED TREE

Assuming you have chosen your first potensai from a bonsai nursery or garden centre, it can be initially styled using a stout pair of scissors, a decent pair of sharp secateurs, a pair of pliers capable of cutting wire and two or three different grades of wire.

Find a comfortable place to work where you will not be disturbed for a couple of hours (you will be amazed at how quickly time passes when engrossed with a tree) and examine the plant from all angles to decide on the best aspect to form the front. Look for the most interesting trunk line, good taper and reasonable branch placement. If the tree is overpotted, scrape away the surface compost until you find the roots, if necessary cutting a couple of inches from the rim of the pot to allow you to see the whole trunk line from roots to apex. Mark your chosen front with a stick or pencil near the pot rim. If it is difficult to see the trunk because of the number of branches (as is often the case with bushy-growing conifers), begin removing some that will definitely not be required in the design, such as thick, heavy branches near the apex, weak, spindly lower branches and those growing straight forward out of the prospective front.

You do not have to settle for a straight trunk – like branches, these can be shaped with wire – nor does the trunk angle have to be the same as in the pot. Try propping the pot at different angles to see the effect on the overall image, and if you find an angle that seems to work, secure it at that angle and style the tree around the lean produced.

The next step is to reduce the tree down to its bare essentials; leaving only those branches that are best placed or that can be wired into a better position for the envisaged design. By now, you should have a vague idea of the style the tree will become; if not, informal upright is a relatively safe bet. Remember a tree that has undergone initial styling is by no means finished, in fact quite the reverse, it is just beginning life as a bonsai and what are now spindly, sparsely-foliaged branches can thicken up and fill out enormously in a few years. Trying to picture what a tree can become is where the real art of bonsai comes in. Bonsai masters are able to look at relatively unpromising material, prune back to only a few branches while

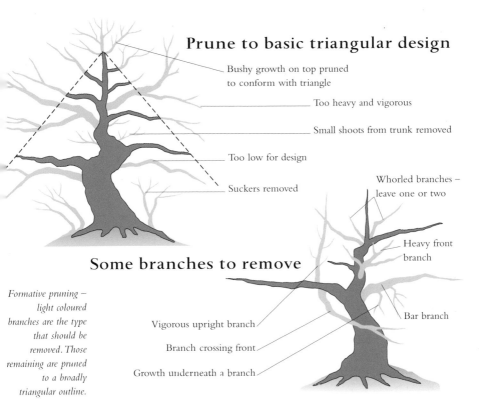

Prune to basic triangular design

Bushy growth on top pruned
to conform with triangle

Too heavy and vigorous

Small shoots from trunk removed

Too low for design

Suckers removed

Whorled branches –
leave one or two

Heavy front
branch

Bar branch

Some branches to remove

*Formative pruning –
light coloured
branches are the type
that should be
removed. Those
remaining are pruned
to a broadly
triangular outline.*

Vigorous upright branch

Branch crossing front

Growth underneath a branch

envisaging not only how the same tree can be made to look in five, ten or even twenty years time, but precisely how to mould the emerging new branches and foliage over the course of this period. Such visual forward planning does not come naturally. To an extent it comes with experience and practice, but in another way it is the true artistry of bonsai, and not something that can be taught. Like great painters, bonsai masters are born, not made.

Branch selection

There is no single formula for good branch structure in bonsai. Deciding on which branches to remove and which to retain is always subjective, unless the tree has very few. The most important guidelines are that the lowest branches should usually be the heaviest and most widely spaced, becoming closer together, thinner and more crowded further up the trunk. Select the lowest branch first since its characteristics will have a bearing on the others selected. Ideally it should be to the right or left of the main trunk, not behind. If the lower branches are all relatively thin, which often occurs as they are shaded by more vigorous ones higher up, they can be allowed free rein to thicken up while the rest of the tree is kept more tightly pruned and cut back to scale later. This is also a useful technique for thickening up the lower part of the trunk and improving taper. Sometimes a grower will leave several lower branches just to develop a more powerful trunk base, and remove all or all but one once the desired thickening has taken place. The stubs of such 'sacrifice' branches can be converted into deadwood or jins, but given the scarring that hard pruning can cause, try to ensure sacrifice branches emerge from the back of the tree.

Working up from the first branch, the next should ideally be placed higher up on the opposite side of the trunk, and the third towards the back. A common mistake for beginners is to train a two-dimensional, 'flat' tree. Back branches are fundamental to giving a tree depth and most designs require at least one. Working your way up the tree, try to select progressively thinner branches closer and closer together, while keeping a sequence of right, left, to rear. If a branch at a particular point is too thin compared to ones higher up, again it can be allowed to grow on and thicken. Avoid placing branches on the insides of curves in the trunk, remove any that cross, and where branches emerge from the same point in whorls, retain only the best placed. Towards the apex of the tree, this is less critical and two or even three can be retained. Try to think in terms of using the branches as a base for clouds, or levels of foliage, leaving enough of a gap between them to accommodate this foliage, while still allowing the gaps, or negative areas, between branches to give a tree-like, rather than a shrubby, image.

With deciduous material and most broad-leaved evergreens, if you decide you have cut off the wrong branch, don't despair as such species will often produce new shoots around pruning cuts. Conifers must be treated slightly differently as budding back on older wood is much less likely. Conifer branches also need to have at least some foliage on them to continue drawing sap – in most species, if a branch is completely defoliated it will die back. When branch pruning resinous species, such as pines and spruces, it is better to leave a short stub than cut flush to the trunk, which may otherwise weep resin for months.

Once the stub has died back and the bark on it has dried, it can be cut back to the bole.

The cone of vigour

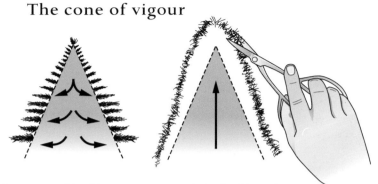

Invert the natural cone of vigour (left) by pruning the upper parts of the tree hard (right).

One way of looking at tree growth is the idea of a 'cone of vigour' (above). Young trees tend to exhibit strong apical dominance, that is, the topmost shoots grow the most strongly as the young plant grows towards the light and increases its height as quickly as possible. In bonsai this is a problem as a tree left to its own devices will bush at the top, and the branches there will thicken at the expense of the lower ones. Since we are striving to produce images of full sized trees, whose lower branches are invariably the largest, we are actually trying to invert the natural cone of vigour and produce the most growth lowest down. The answer is to prune hard in the upper parts of the tree, which effectively diverts growth hormones and sugars to lower, more lightly pruned areas. This is particularly important in the initial styling of a tree, but is also fundamental to its subsequent development.

The apex of the tree is often the most difficult part to style convincingly. If the main trunk line or leader is still relatively thick, a common and usually successful ploy is to cut it back to just above a suitable side branch, which can then be trained upright to replace it. This is also a way to shorten trees substantially and any obvious change in taper will soon disappear as scar tissue forms around the wound. Don't be afraid of drastically shortening potensai by half or even two-thirds if the lower branches are suitable, as the tree will immediately look thicker, chunkier – and therefore older. In the upper parts of the tree, branches that project forward are acceptable, and pruning to a forward-facing side branch has the advantage of hiding the scar that leader removal produces. If the branches along the lower two-thirds of the trunk have been decided on and any thick or crossing ones removed from the apex, it is often easier to proceed to the wiring stage, leaving the styling of the apex to the end of the process.

Wiring

Aside from pruning, wiring is probably the most important method of shaping a tree, and it is worth practising its application on dead sticks and twigs before tackling your first bonsai. Wire should be wound in equidistant coils at approximately 45 degrees along a branch, but not applied so tightly that it cuts into the bark immediately – the idea is to hold the branch firmly but not to straitjacket it.

Traditionally, annealed (heated and cooled, therefore soft) copper wire was used. Once applied, exposure to the elements makes copper progressively stiffer which, while it helps to hold the branch firmly, makes it more difficult to remove. Copper has been largely superceded in bonsai by aluminium wire, often given a brown surface to help it tone in. Although not as strong as copper, meaning it has to be thicker, aluminium is easy to work with and apply. Steel or iron is not suitable as it rusts and stains the bark, but plastic-coated steel can be used with care and is more freely available than aluminium wire, which may have to be sourced from a specialist bonsai nursery or mail order supplier.

The thickness of wire needed to hold a trunk or branch varies from species to species (and even between individuals of the same species); if in doubt err on the side of caution and apply a relatively thin gauge of wire. If this is not enough to hold the limb in position, apply a second coil of the same gauge and this should hold it. Many bonsai texts advise the wiring of every single branch and twig, but I would not advocate this for novices. Hone your application skills on trunks and thick branches first, and only then begin to tackle the really fine, fiddly twigs. Your initial structural pruning should have given you an idea of the tree's flexibility – see how far you can bend the discarded branches without them snapping or their bark separating from the wood. Species like junipers are usually fairly flexible while other species such as azaleas are brittle and snap easily, so can only be wired when young and flexible.

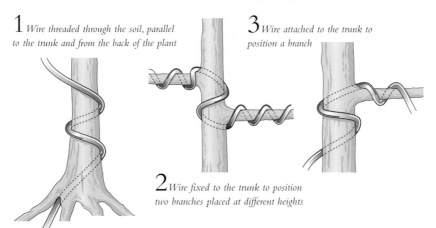

1 *Wire threaded through the soil, parallel to the trunk and from the back of the plant*

3 *Wire attached to the trunk to position a branch*

2 *Wire fixed to the trunk to position two branches placed at different heights*

The single most important factor in wiring a tree is to make sure every piece of wire applied is well anchored, otherwise it will never hold its position. To wire a trunk, push one end of the wire deep into the rootball before starting to coil (above, left), and when wiring branches, either take a couple of turns around the trunk first (above, right) or anchor the wire to another branch. Alternatively, wire branches in pairs and they will anchor each other (above, centre). Cut a piece at least half as long again as the branch or branches to be wired – it is better to be left with an excess that can be trimmed back than to come up short. The main branches of a mature tree rarely have much foliage close to the trunk due to shading, so remove any such foliage and any pointing down below the branch before applying the wire.

Wiring for overall shape

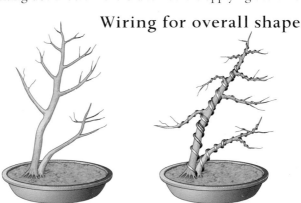

Wiring upward growing branches lower immediately makes a juvenile tree look older.

Wiring

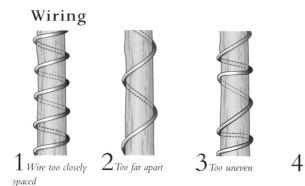
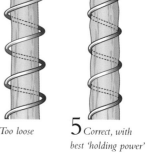

1 *Wire too closely spaced* 2 *Too far apart* 3 *Too uneven* 4 *Too loose* 5 *Correct, with best 'holding power'*

If you want to improve a straight trunk, wire this first. Coil a suitably thick piece of wire neatly up the trunk from base to tip, at approximately 45 degrees and spaced 1cm (½in) or so apart. Have an idea of the shape you want to produce, avoiding regular S curves, which have become something of a bonsai cliché, and ideally introducing some movement back to front rather than just side to side, making the apex 'bow' slightly to the front to increase apparent perspective. The technique for bending is the same for trunks and branches. Grip the area to be bent in both hands, your thumbs supporting the inside of the intended curve. Exert pressure slowly and methodically and if you hear any creaks or snapping noises, stop immediately. If the wire proves to be too weak to hold the area in its new shape, apply a second piece of the same gauge. A word of warning: try to avoid bending the same area in different directions in search of the most pleasing shape, as this puts stress on the living cells just below the bark, which can disrupt the flow of sap and the branch may die. Decide on the form first and stick to it.

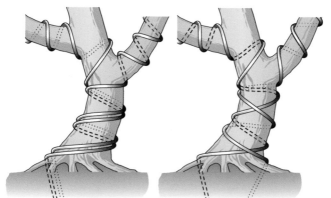

Left: The correct way to double wire a trunk. The wires can then be split to hold the lowest two branches.

Right: Crossing wires not only put undue stress on the points where they overlap, they also have little holding power.

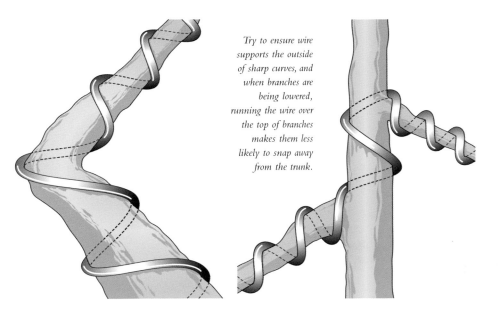

Try to ensure wire supports the outside of sharp curves, and when branches are being lowered, running the wire over the top of branches makes them less likely to snap away from the trunk.

It is usually easiest to begin by bending the trunk and the first branch, since these largely set the style of the tree. I would not advocate the novice trying to introduce very abrupt curves in their first few trees, but if you want to attempt it later, wrap the area to be bent before wiring with several layers of raffia, then wire and bend. Even if the wood snaps, the raffia should keep the all-important bark together rather than it splintering. This is also a useful method to protect the thin or delicate bark of species such as Japanese maples and azaleas from damage caused by the wire itself.

On a young tree, most of the branches will probably be growing upwards, so the main aim of wiring is to bring them down closer to the horizontal as in an older tree (p.53). Place the first few coils around the branch relatively closely together, and ensure the wire runs over the upper part of the branch junction rather than underneath it, as this makes snapping less likely (above). Greater depth to the design can be introduced by curving the branch carefully away and slightly towards the viewer. One of the best ways of making a bonsai's design work is to train the branches to similar shapes. A slightly concave branch, descending a little from the trunk to rise a little towards

The neon-bright colouring of this spindle, Euonymus alatus, *is typical of its genus and explains the choice of the blush-pink of its pot.*

the tip will look like it is 'cupping' the foliage. This is a common branch profile well-suited to small-leaved species such as junipers and cotoneasters. Spruces and firs usually have their branches trained slightly downwards and straight to mimic their natural pyramidal form, whereas pines are often given fairly abrupt twists and turns, so shortening their long, straight branches, with growing tips trained upwards to mimic their natural growth form. Straight, curved, concave or convex, the important thing is that all the branches should be given similar characteristics. Look at trees in the wild and you will see why – although branching is influenced by climate and exposure, a large proportion of its pattern is genetically programmed into each individual tree.

Branch profiles

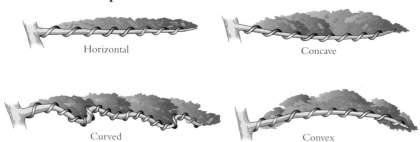

Horizontal

Concave

Curved

Convex

Work your way up the tree from the lowest branch, placing each in turn into their most pleasing position. Thin out and remove foliage and sub-branches that fall below major branches and those that project straight up or are too large, but don't worry too much about the fine structure of the remaining thin sub-branches at this stage. Don't be afraid to twist wired branches slightly to bring the foliage above their line. Keep stepping back from the tree and looking at it from a distance, and examine it from the sides and back, as well as from the front.

When looking from above, place branches in a spiral pattern around the trunk so that no major branch is directly over a lower one and there is at least one major back branch. Make slight adjustments as you go along so that each branch is worked into the overall design. Approximately two-thirds of the way up the trunk, foliage can begin to be brought in front of the trunk.

Having styled the rest of the tree, the apex can now be formed to blend in with it. Some bonsai enthusiasts advocate training the top of a tree first, but I have always found it easier to do the reverse. There is usually quite a choice of thin, twiggy growth at the apex once any heavy branches and the original leader have been pruned, and you will have a better idea of how much it needs to be reduced when the rest of the tree has been initially styled. As the apex is usually the most vigorous part of the tree, don't be afraid to cut it back relatively hard. If you have

This wire is just beginning to 'bite' into the branch and should be removed to avoid scarring.

cut back the leader, wire a replacement into an upright position or a position that harmonizes with the lower trunk line. Decide which twigs are best removed, such as crossing ones, shoots growing straight up or down and those projecting straight forward. In most designs, a relatively rounded head is preferable.

Once you have finished wiring and pruning, step back and assess the overall image and make any minor adjustments necessary. It can help to go away and do something else for a couple of hours then come back for a final assessment. If you are happy with the result – and again bear in mind this is only the initial styling and the tree may look very different with a few years' growth – water it well, give it a spray from a mister and place it in a sheltered, shaded spot in the garden to recover. If you are styling a dormant tree in autumn, a cold porch or unheated glasshouse may be preferable in colder areas, as pruning wounds are vulnerable to frost damage.

Potting

Don't be in too much of a hurry to repot a newly styled bonsai. Allow it at least a couple of weeks recuperation to get over the shock in autumn or winter, or repot the following spring. If the tree was styled while in active growth, leave repotting until it is dormant in the autumn. You can often get away with transferring a newly styled container-grown tree into a bonsai pot straight away but it is heartbreaking to lose a newly styled tree, with real potential, to your own impatience. Unless you are transferring a tree into a larger training pot, therefore, it is usually better to see how the plant responds to its styling before attacking its rootball too. Potting up a newly styled bonsai is exactly the same as repotting a trained tree, which is covered in the maintenance and refinement section (see p.70).

On the subject of pots, trees respond much more quickly to training with space for root growth, so to develop a bonsai quickly, pot it up in a large training pot or plant it into the ground – the difference in growth rates between these and trees in their final display pots can be astonishing. Display pots are really for trees that have gone beyond their initial styling. Each is chosen to fit the style and character of its tree like a frame matched to a painting, and are best employed when refining the image by encouraging fine, twiggy growth is more important than building up bulk. The rockery or other suitable spaces in the garden are excellent for growing on stock that needs 'fattening up', or for planting out material with which styling has been less than successful. After a couple of years in the ground and minimal attention, a completely different tree with different design possibilities usually emerges.

Training 'Specials'

Some styles of bonsai, most notably rock plantings, are formed by their own additional training methods, as is the creation and treatment of deadwood, which can be used on many different styles of tree. Their overall shape is produced by the same methods already discussed.

Jins and sharis

As mentioned (see p. 25), jins are dead, broken branches and sharis dead, bleached areas of trunk. Although probably overused, in the right context both can be powerful tools for making a tree look as if it has been exposed to the elements and make it appear older as a result. Jins can also be a better way of dealing with a branch that has been removed than a major pruning wound. The bare wood of trees with natural wounds or die-back has usually been bleached and smoothed by

exposure to wind and weather, and often shows intricate patterns of graining – all of which can be produced artificially. Perhaps the greatest natural examples of bonsai's driftwood style are the immensely ancient bristlecone pines of California, the oldest examples of which are well into their fifth millennium, and primarily made up of twisted and contorted dead trunks on which a few branches can be found, clinging tenaciously to life. Driftwood-style trees with extensive areas of shari are almost always coniferous, as the wood of broad-leaved trees is not so resistant to decay so tends to fall off the

A selection of 'tools of the trade' at a bonsai nursery. By no means essential, they do make life easier for the committed grower.

tree relatively quickly. However, jins and hollow scars suggesting shed branches, in Japanese 'uros', are appropriate methods of disguising pruning cuts in several deciduous species. One exception to this norm include the olive, old specimens of which are commonly half-decayed or even completely hollow yet still vigorous, and occasional hawthorns (right).

Jins and sharis are not difficult to create, it is simply a case of peeling the bark from an area, carving it if necessary and preserving it. To make a jin, roughly snap off the branch to the required length, ring its base by cutting through to the wood, then peel off the bark. If it is alive, the bark should come away relatively easily. Thin jins can look ridiculous, so the technique is best applied to relatively thick branches. Alternatively, peel the bark without ringing it and you will usually tear the bark below the branch, making a shari. It is best to decide exactly where you want a shari by drawing it on the trunk, then cutting around the area with a craft knife or scalpel, or you may end up stripping too big an area. To get the most natural look to a jin, crush the broken end with a pair of pliers and peel away thin strips to expose the internal graining. Avoid unnatural 'pencil point' shapes. If the branch has just been stripped, it should be flexible enough to wire into a better shape if necessary; or, if the branch can be gently heated with a flame (without damaging nearby foliage), it becomes flexible enough to be easily bent into a new shape. Hold it in this position until it has cooled and, remarkably, it will stay there. Using a blowtorch, really thick pieces of deadwood can be bent by this method.

Allow newly created jins and sharis several weeks to dry and they can then be further carved to suggest graining or decayed areas, either by hand with small chisels or woodcarving tools, or with router attachments on a craft drill (a peculiarly satisfying procedure). Aim for natural-looking shapes rather than abstract ones. Once you have the jin or shari carved to your satisfaction, it needs preserving. The traditional Japanese method is lime-sulphur, a foul-smelling yellow concoction that bleaches as well as preserves. This is available from specialist bonsai suppliers but beware – not only does it smell of rotten eggs, it can dissolve the bristles of some brushes. If the resulting silver or white colour seems too stark, try adding a few drops of grey paint or black ink to the lime sulphur, which will tone it down.

An excellent example of naturalistic carving on a hawthorn, Crataegus monogyna, *suggesting a tree battered by the elements but unbowed.*

Rock plantings

Ishitsuki, or 'clinging to rock' style, and sekijoju, or 'root over rock', have their own special techniques, primarily concerned with the initial attachment of the plant. Both depend on finding suitable pieces of rock, whether from nature (riversides, beaches and craggy areas) or the garden centre. Steer clear of water-worn limestone which, although nicely weathered, has

A method of attachment for clinging to rock where there is no planting pocket

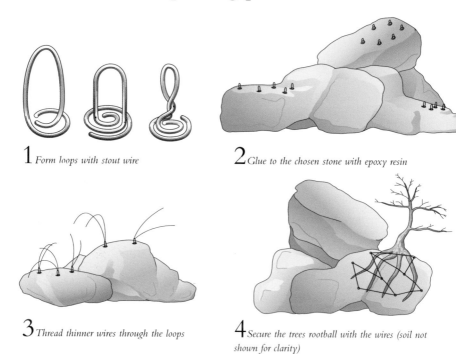

1 *Form loops with stout wire*

2 *Glue to the chosen stone with epoxy resin*

3 *Thread thinner wires through the loops*

4 *Secure the trees rootball with the wires (soil not shown for clarity)*

usually been taken from limestone pavements, an increasingly rare natural habitat. Choose a visually interesting, well-textured piece that will complement the colours of the tree you want to plant with it. Tufa is an excellent choice for ishitsuki as it is relatively soft, allowing suitable planting pockets to be carved out (and a flat, stable base to be formed) as well as porous, allowing excess water to drain away.

Dramatic, craggy rocks are a major feature of pen-jing, and there is a whole industry in China devoted to assembling miniature crags from pieces of limestone to echo the sugar-loaf, near vertical, karst limestone scenery of the area. These are often offered for sale in specialist bonsai nurseries and although quite expensive due to their weight, make excellent bases for clinging to rock plantings, with the other advantage of being deliberately made with a flat base. Alternatively, have a go yourself by sticking together smaller rocks with epoxy resin or car filler paste.

Once planted, tree and stone are going to remain as one unit, so make the planting pocket large enough to support the tree long-term or else choose a stone that will blend with a tree sat proud of it on a 'dome' of compost. Given the amount of root disturbance involved, it is best to assemble these rock plantings in autumn or early spring while the tree is dormant. On a harder stone, or if you want to plant on the side of a rock, glue several loops of wire firmly to the stone with epoxy resin glue around the area to be planted and allow them to dry.

This root over rock Japanese maple is exceptional for the way its roots convincingly grip the rock surface and the way its trunk follows the line of the rock.

Ishitsuki plantings are often made using very small trees, as for maximum effect the rock should be the dominant part of the composition, suggesting a crag or cliff-face in the distance with correspondingly small tree shapes. Really dwarf conifers such as firs, spruces and some selections of pine, such as *Pinus mugo* 'Mops' are good choices, as is *Chamaecyparis obtusa* 'Nana Gracilis'. Many dwarf selections are grafted, however, and the bulge of a bad graft will be just as visible on a small trunk as on a larger one, so choose carefully.

Roughly shape your chosen plant according to where you are going to place it, removing unwanted foliage, and wire the main branches. If you are placing more than one tree on a rock, make it an odd number, and try each in the different planting positions to find the best match. Next, tease out as much of the compost from the outer rootball as possible and prune off the long roots, also scraping away the upper layers to expose the surface roots if they are going to be visible. Because they are planted in such small pockets of soil, rock plantings tend to dry out quickly, so the planting medium is made more water-retentive than usual — traditionally a 50-50 mix of peat or peat substitute and loam or John Innes compost. Adding a little pure clay helps moisture retention further.

Thread wires between the loops attached to the stone, then line the base of the planting pocket with a little compost mixture. Introduce the pruned rootball and firm more mixture around the roots, adjusting the tree to give the best trunk angle, then secure the tree in position with the wires. Now add a little more soil to cover the wires and loops. You can further secure the surface by stretching an old piece of stocking or tights over it, but either way the whole compost surface should be covered with pieces of moss secured with loops of thin wire. This not only retains moisture but also prevents compost from being washed away during watering.

Once the tree has been well secured, give it its final shaping, taking into account its relationship with the rock. On steep-sided rocks, cascade style is proably the most obvious, but don't ignore other dramatic styles such as windswept and slanting, which help conjure the image of an exposed mountain peak.

Rock plantings are traditionally displayed in shallow water dishes known as tsuiban, making them look like mini islands and, more importantly, keeping the humidity up and reducing water loss. Ceramic tsuiban are difficult to source but a shallow plastic tray will do as an alternative. A handful of gravel (in a complementary colour) around the base of the rock giving way to a clean dish immediately makes the mind think 'beach', reinforcing the island image.

A good way of reducing watering and keeping rock plantings looking their best, at least over the warmer months, is to push a strip of capillary matting into the back of each planting pocket and lead it down the back of the rock into the water below. The tree is then able to take up as much water as it needs. Remove the matting strips at the onset of winter or you may get waterlogging problems. Rock plantings tend to be more vulnerable to frozen rootballs than trees growing in bonsai pots, so overwintering in a frost-free porch or cold greenhouse, away from drying winds, is recommended.

Root over rock (sekijoju)

This style is such a dramatic one, most beginners cannot wait to try it out, and it is neither particularly difficult nor time consuming to initiate. It does involve the complete removal of compost from a tree's root system, however, which is a major shock to its system. This should only be attempted with vigorous stock that has already recovered from a severe reduction in top growth, and is best limited to early spring unless an area is available for winter protection. The most common species used is the Japanese trident maple, but many other species are suitable providing they produce a relatively thick and robust root system. Aside from trident maples, my favourite subjects for root over rock are junipers. The style is also suited to trees that have just not made it as convincing trees in other styles. Training a tree over a rock can make a poor bonsai look much better, but it will never be a classic. The best sekijoju are undoubtedly those where the tree and rock have been chosen to complement each other, so that from a distance they look like a bonsai with an outsized but dramatic trunk, and on closer observation the individual roots sweep down over the rock in fluid lines before entering the soil.

Container-grown stock often has long roots coiled up in the pot so is a good bet for root over rock starter material. Many sources advocate raising plants from seed in exceptionally deep cascade type pots, or even thick cardboard tubes plunged into the soil, but it will be several years before the tree is anything like ready to train. Unless you have chosen a particularly tall rock, all that is needed is a tree with roots long enough to go down the side of the rock and into the compost, so an average 3 litre pot should prove ample for your purposes.

In good root over rock specimens, the rock is at least as important as the tree and, if it is intended to be larger than the tree, perhaps more so. You can influence the shape of the tree once it has established successfully but you can't change the rock. Hard, impermeable rocks such as granite, flint and dolomite are preferable to softer rocks like tufa, which can crumble over time and ruin the composition. Ideally, the rock should have a 'saddle' over which the trunk and rootbase can fit and grooves or fissures running down the areas where the roots are to be trained.

Root over rock: traditional method

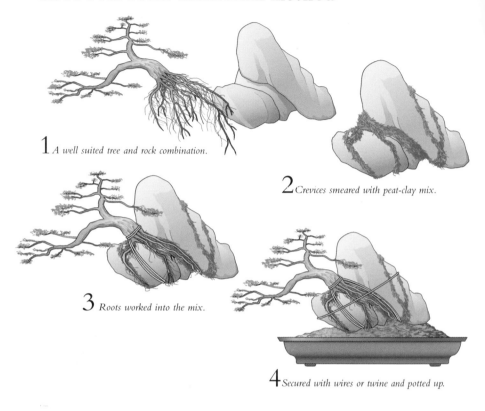

1 *A well suited tree and rock combination.*

2 *Crevices smeared with peat-clay mix.*

3 *Roots worked into the mix.*

4 *Secured with wires or twine and potted up.*

Close up of Acer palmatum *roots over a rock.*

The traditional method for securing the tree to the stone is to carefully hammer in loops of wire, with their ends wrapped in thick lead foil along the channels where the roots are to run, smear the channels with a thin layer of peat-clay mix, then wire the roots tightly to the rock. Epoxy resin is an alternative way to secure the loops but experimentation with more modern materials in the West has produced other options.

Root over rock: tinfoil method

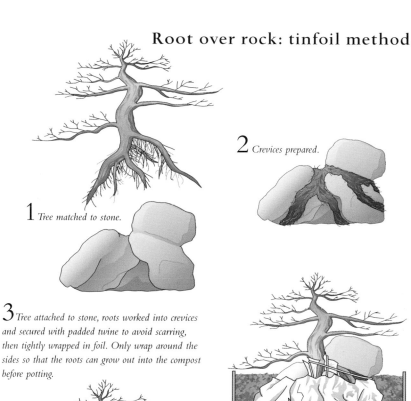

1 *Tree matched to stone.*

2 *Crevices prepared.*

3 *Tree attached to stone, roots worked into crevices and secured with padded twine to avoid scarring, then tightly wrapped in foil. Only wrap around the sides so that the roots can grow out into the compost before potting.*

4 *Assembly potted into a large wooden training box to grow on.*

Given that the roots are going to be the main feature of the planting, choose the area of the most interesting and biggest root formation for the front, unless this makes a major fault in the branches of the tree visible. Decide from the number of channels on the rock and the number of areas into which the main roots fall how many groups of roots you would like to produce. Prepare the rock by working thin channels of peat-clay mix into these and try to spread the channels as evenly as possible around the rock.

If you can, secure the trunk base to its planting saddle using wire loops, as this will make it easier to attach the roots. Working from top to bottom, push the root groups into the peat-clay so that they are close to the rock surface, securing with wires, tape or ties as you go along. It can be a messy, frustrating business, but the final results are usually worth it. You should end up with something like a trussed-up chicken, covered in wire or ties, with lengths of root protruding from the base. Now wrap the whole rock-root combination with thick plastic or foil (both more effective than the traditional sphagnum moss).

The way in which these roots seem to flow down over the rock before plunging into the soil epitomizes the struggle for life sekijoju represents.

With the tree firmly attached to the rock, encourage the roots to expand as quickly as possible so that they adhere to the rock surface, become woody and set in position. The quickest way of doing this is to plant the whole arrangement in the ground, burying most of the stone. Leave it for at least a growing season, preferably two, allowing the branches fairly free rein (without allowing the apex to take over and thicken at the expense of the lower branches). Alternatively, plant into a deep training pot, and again allow free growth for at least a season.

After this growth period, ideally in early spring, examine the planting and if the roots visible at the top of the rock have thickened substantially, lift the whole assemblage and cut away the top 2cm (¾in) or so of the foil or plastic, washing away compost with a fine water spray. If the roots seem to be gripping the rock, cut away a little more, but if not, stop there and pot up the tree to this level. Training of the upper part of the tree so that it harmonizes with the rock can now begin in earnest. At subsequent repottings, you will be able to raise the rock ever higher until you begin to reach its base.

Whichever approach is adopted to creating root over rock, there is no shortcutting the time needed for the roots to grip the rock, and producing a good tree-like image will always take several years. It is therefore one of the best styles for teaching one of bonsai's most important lessons: patience.

Maintenance and Refinement

Placement

Where to grow your bonsai is a major consideration. Ideally they should not be in full sun or heavy shade, but in a semi-shaded spot in the garden, which receives full sun for part of the day. Having invested a great deal of time and trouble in making your trees look good, you will want to display them to their best advantage and this means on some sort of shelving system where they are raised near eye level, not on the ground where they are more exposed to accidental damage and pests. Greenhouse staging is one option but is rarely robust enough to carry more than a few trees. A stout, custom-made system is preferable; breeze blocks and heavy wooden planks are perhaps the easiest, ideally cemented in place against a house wall for protection. If you do use wood, make sure it is either pressure-treated with preservative, or given several coats of wood preservative. Having shelves at different heights will allow you to display different sized trees and, if in doubt, err on the side of giving yourself more space rather than less, as trees look their best given room from their neighbours.

Although your bonsai have definite fronts that will normally face towards you, turn them occasionally to allow all parts of the trees to receive light. Really large bonsai probably look best on their own pedestal or 'monkey pole'. Substantial display stands can also be useful in winter, as trees can be placed under them and the whole unit covered in plastic sheeting or fleece for protection against frost and drying winds.

Stout wooden shelving in a neutral colour is one of the most effective ways to display small and medium-sized bonsai.

70

Purists may argue that that bonsai should only be displayed in a Japanese setting, but I disagree. Plants in containers are an important part of most British gardens, and their inhabitants are drawn from all corners of the world. Bonsai may be exceptional pot plants, but they can look surprisingly at home anywhere.

Many bonsai enthusiasts do nevertheless develop an interest in Japanese gardening as a result of growing bonsai, and even if they only strive for an oriental feel for the immediate vicinity of their display area, this helps set their trees in some sort of

context and means they do not have to directly compete with relatively gaudy 'ordinary' flowering plants. A restful, neutral background can be produced with bamboo or rush screening, and typically Japanese garden items such as interesting rocks or stone lanterns placed around the display area work wonders, as can a simple gravel flooring and a few potted foliage plants such as hostas or grasses. Newly styled trees or those being grown-on can always be sited in a less obtrusive part of the garden.

Acer palmatum 'Sango-kaku', the coral bark maple, is best known for its shrimp-pink young shoots, but can also produce exceptional autumn colour.

If you must grow indoor bonsai, give them as much light as possible close to a window, well away from sources of heat like radiators or electrical equipment: central heating and tropical or sub-tropical plants do not mix well. Neither do indoor bonsai like cold, so if they are on a windowsill make sure the window is a close-fitting one with no cold draughts, and if closing the curtains do not leave the tree between curtain and glass. Standing indoor bonsai in a shallow dish of gravel kept constantly damp will help raise the humidity around it, but even so, watch the watering like a hawk – a single drying out can be fatal with some of the most commonly offered species.

Watering

Apprentices in Japanese bonsai nurseries used to spend the first two years of their five- or six-year apprenticeship doing nothing but watering, an indication of how important the process is. In summer, your trees will probably need to be watered at least once a day, depending on their size and prevailing weather conditions. It is good practice anyway to check your trees daily for watering and to keep an eye out for pests and diseases that may require treatment (p.75). Just because it has rained, don't assume your bonsai have had enough water - they are in small pots, much of the surface of which is overhung with foliage. Assessing whether a tree requires watering can be difficult, particularly if the soil surface has a covering of moss or gravel, so keep an unobtrusive area of the compost surface clear to allow a visual check for dryness. With smaller bonsai, the best way of assessing water requirements is by weight. Feel the weight of the tree and pot in your hand straight after watering and compare the difference when it is dry.

To avoid disturbing the compost surface, particularly with newly potted trees, watering needs to be gentle, either using a watering can with a fine rose, or a hose with a fine spray connected to a slow-running tap. Water each tree well in turn until water runs out of the drainage hole in the pot, then go back to the beginning and water each again. Small bonsai and rock plantings in particular dry out quickly and may need watering morning and night during hot spells in the summer. Most outdoor trees also enjoy a splash of water over their foliage to clean and refresh them, but never do this in full sun as the drops of water can act like lenses and scorch the foliage. For a thorough watering, or if a tree has got really dry, immerse its pot completely in a bucket or dish of water for five or ten minutes.

With deciduous trees, the maximum demand for water is likely to be spring, when their new leaves are forming, rather than summer, but the water requirement for all species goes up when in active growth. Evergreens in particular need water in late autumn and winter also, so keep checking them even when the weather is cold. Bonsai are small plants in small pots and in very cold periods, their pots can freeze completely. Even with fully hardy species that can withstand the lower temperatures, if freezing conditions are combined with strong winds the roots are unable to supply water to the tree, while the wind continues to strip moisture from the leaves and branches. Losing bonsai to weather conditions can be heartbreaking, but it is rarely absolute cold that kills them, it is the freeze-drying of cold combined with wind.

Sheltering the trees under the stand is one way of keeping them out of the wind, or moving them into protected areas such as cold greenhouses, porches, or even dark sheds and garages for short periods. Cold snaps in spring can also be damaging to vulnerable emerging foliage, so on cold nights be prepared to bring trees indoors that are leafing. Borderline species that have been overwintered under cover need to be hardened off gradually to outside conditions, putting them out on still, relatively warm days but bringing them back in for the night or if cold winds threaten.

Feeding

Ask ten different bonsai growers how they feed their trees and you will get ten different answers; like potting mixes each has their own preference. One fairly foolproof method is to mix in slow-release fertilizer granules when formulating the growing medium, as these break down slowly and release nutrients gradually over a year. They can also be scattered over the compost surface, but avoid areas of decorative moss as the nutrient concentrations are too much for it. Alternatively, add a weak liquid feed once a week while your trees are growing actively. Flowering species such as cherries and crabapples appreciate higher levels of potash, such as that found in tomato feed (but not when they are actually in flower), while ericaceous plants that like acid conditions such as azaleas (rhododendron species) should be given a specially formulated ericaceous feed with sequestered iron and no lime. For trees in initial training that are being encouraged to bulk up, regular sprays of foliar feeds build vigour.

Don't use a high nitrogen feed in autumn, as it will merely encourage weak, sappy growth that has less chance of surviving the winter. A specialist 0-10-10 (N:P:K) formulation feed in autumn with no nitrogen helps 'harden off' the year's new wood in preparation for winter.

Pests and diseases

Bonsai are attacked by the same pests and diseases as their full-sized counterparts, but because of their smaller stature, they are more vulnerable and can be badly affected by outbreaks. A single caterpillar can virtually defoliate a small tree overnight (but is usually easy to spot and can be removed by hand), and sap-sucking pests like aphids can cause young emerging foliage to distort. Some species are prone to fungal diseases that attack the foliage such as mildews, and all can suffer from root rots, particularly if overwatered and potted into too heavy a compost. Keeping your trees off the ground gives a measure of protection from ground-dwelling pests such as slugs and snails (and makes them less likely to be knocked over), but is little protection from public enemy number one, the vine weevil. Get into the habit of checking your trees regularly for pests and diseases, including the undersides of leaves, as problems are much easier to treat at an early stage. If a chemical treatment is necessary, read the label and follow the instructions to the letter. Space unfortunately precludes a more detailed look at anything but the most commonly encountered problems.

Pests

Vine weevils are unattractive, long-snouted beetles that cannot fly, but are the mountaineers of the insect world. They are largely nocturnal, and the first signs of their presence is usually ragged, irregular notches eaten out of the edges of leaves, particularly those of broad leaved evergreens. It is their larvae that are the real danger, however, as these live underground and feed on the roots of a wide range of plants. In the confines of a pot, they are quite capable of killing even quite substantial trees. If the characteristic notched leaves appear anywhere in the garden or on your bonsai, or if you find fat white grubs up to 2cm ($^3/_4$ in) long with a brown head during repotting, treatment is a must. The only option used to be a biological control using a parasitic nematode worm, but this could only be used in summer when soil temperatures were high. Fortunately a new pesticide, imidachloprid, is available (Bio Provado), that can be diluted and used to drench the soil. This is also a systemic insecticide, meaning it is taken up by the plants' roots and transported up to the leaves, where it will also poison any sap-sucking insects.

The most prevalent sap-sucking species are aphids (greenfly and blackfly), most common on the young leaves of deciduous trees. When feeding, they often secrete a sticky substance called honeydew that drips onto the leaves below, which can quickly become colonized by an unattractive black sooty mould. Their equivalent in coniferous trees, particularly pines, are adelgids, fluffy white insects that feed well down in the foliage. Red spider mite, formerly only found in glasshouses, is being recorded out of doors more frequently, and is also the biggest problem on indoor bonsai. The mites themselves are tiny, but their feeding causes leaves to be mottled yellow and fall early. The other tell-tale sign is a fine white webbing on leaves or branches that the mites secrete for protection. Regularly misting the foliage can keep spider mite in check as they prefer dry conditions. The chemical solution to all these problems is to spray with a systemic insecticide (read the label for information on which insect species it controls). Organic controls include washing pests away with a jet of water, or spraying with a product based on soft soap or fatty acids, paying particular attention to the undersides of the leaves. More than one treatment may be necessary for serious infestations.

Diseases

Leaf-affecting diseases such as mildews (white, powdery film on leaves), rusts (reddish spots, particularly on the underside of leaves) and scabs (larger, irregularly-shaped brown areas particularly common on crab apples) can all usually be dealt with by a spray with a systemic fungicide (again, check the label for the specific diseases controlled). The organic alternative is a formulation based on sulphur, usually applied as a powder, or copper sulphate, such as Bordeaux mixture. Alternatively, pick off and dispose of affected leaves promptly, which will help stop the problem spreading.

The most serious wood-affecting disease is probably coral spot, a fungus that gains entry through wounds and pruning cuts. It is characterized by tiny bright orange 'pimples' on the bark, and there is no effective treatment other than to prune out the affected part of the tree, cutting back several centimetres into healthy wood below the infection.

Root rots can be difficult to diagnose, but if a tree begins to wilt and its foliage to yellow even when it is wet, there may well be problems with the roots. Prevention, by using a free-draining compost mix and not overwatering, is better than cure, but if a tree shows these symptoms, remove it from its pot and check the roots. Any that are soft, black or dark brown should be pruned away and the tree repotted into a more open compost mix. This is a shock to the system for an already weak tree, and is a last resort procedure. Keep it in a sheltered, shaded spot, remove some of the foliage to reduce demands on the root system, mist regularly and cross your fingers that it will recover.

REMOVING WIRE AND BONSAI TOOLS

Check regularly how tight the wire has become on trees in training, particularly in spring when decidouous species are growing away strongly. Even newly applied wire can begin to 'bite' into thickening branches in as little as a fortnight and if this is not loosened or removed can badly scar the bark. Spiral wiring scars can take years to fade and in some species may always be obvious. It is usually the part of the branch closest to the trunk that thickens first, so it is sometimes possible to remove the first few turns of wire to ease pressure here, leaving the rest of the branch wired a little longer. If the branch has not set in position, it can be carefully re-wired, avoiding areas covered by the first wiring.

Wire left too long restricts thickening branches, digging into the bark and causing spiral scarring

Almost all bonsai literature advises cutting off the wire rather than attempting to unwind it from a branch and there are certainly occasions when this may be the best option, particularly if the wire has dug in, the area is a congested one or the species has brittle wood. In many other cases, it is perfectly possible to unwind the wire, however, taking care not to bend the branch or take off buds or foliage. Cutting the wire off requires a specialist pair of bonsai wire cutters that cut right to the tip, and even these must be used carefully to avoid cutting into the bark.

A branch badly scarred by wire. This kind of damage takes years to fade, and in some cases never will, remaining a visible fault.

Species with flexible wood-like pines and junipers can take much longer to 'set' into their wired position than deciduous trees, easily more than a year, so the wire may have to be removed and re-applied several times to avoid scarring. The branches of some species also have a tendency to try and adopt a more upright position over time, so wire may need to be applied again to correct the shape several years later.

Aside from wire cutters, the other main tool that is a must for those who are sure bonsai is for them is a pair of side-branch cutters. Essentially a modified pair of precision secateurs with their cutting face at a 45 degree angle, they allow the grower to cut branches flush with the trunk much more easily than with straight secateurs and are also good for hollowing out scars so they heal flush. Keep them sharp, and never use them to cut wire as this is the quickest way to ruin their cutting surfaces. A decent pair of bonsai shears (a special form of scissors) are also useful for cutting both roots and branches, and a pair of longer-handled small scissors will help to get inside the canopy for fine branches and leaves.

MAINTENANCE AND REFINEMENT PRUNING

Initial styling is merely the start of the development of a tree as a bonsai; more regular pruning will fill out, refine and ultimately form the complete image. Particularly with newly styled trees, the focus of developmental pruning should remain reversing the cone of vigour. New shoots that form on the apex should be constantly trimmed short, usually leaving only one or two pairs of leaves on the plant. On branches in the middle of the tree, three or four pairs can be left, with the lowest branches either left completely unpruned if they are being given free rein to thicken up, or just tipped back if the branch needs to be extended. A degree of redirection is also useful on material that has been planted into the ground to thicken up, with the top of the tree again cut back harder than the lower branches to prevent the top growth from becoming too heavy. Since it does not matter what shape sacrifice branches adopt, as they will ultimately be removed, leave them unpruned.

Shoots growing straight up or straight down from any part of the tree should be cut back to their bases, unless they can be wired into position. Particularly with deciduous species, it is possible to prune at the bud stage, simply rubbing off badly placed buds or nipping them out with the fingernails. It is usually obvious which direction a bud will grow in; those swelling to point straight up, down, or in towards the trunk, or forming around scars where branches have been removed, in branch forks or below existing branches, can all be taken off.

Actual pruning techniques vary from species to species (and individual to individual). The particular characteristics of different genera are beyond the remits of such a short text, other than generalizations for some coniferous trees, most notably pines. All species of pine produce needles in whorls around their shoots, and usually have a single growth spurt a year in spring, producing upright new shoots called 'candles'. These appear at the tips of branches, usually in groups of two or three, and left unpruned will concentrate growth in the apex at the expense of other areas. It is obvious which are the most vigorous as they are the longest. As they start to lengthen in spring, and the individual needles start to form down their sides, but before the individual needles start to form, take each

The lengthening shoots of this juniper are beginning to obscure the definition of its foliage clouds, indicating it is time to prune.

candle gently between thumb and forefinger and twist. The candle should break cleanly; do not pull away from the branch or you will snap off the whole thing. At the apex, twist off about two-thirds of each candle and, if the groups are in three or more, remove the largest entirely. In the midsection of the tree, unless you want to extend some of the branches, remove about half of each candle. In the lowest sections, just take off the tips of vigorous candles and, if they are small, leave them unpruned.

It is best to stagger the timing of candle pruning, hitting the top of the tree first, the middle several days later and the lowest parts up to a fortnight later. This has the effect of pushing vigour into the lower branches at the expense of the apex. The aim of candle pruning is to override the pine's natural tendency to concentrate growth in only a few shoots. Wounding the candles by twisting their ends off encourages the formation of more buds, not just at the ends of shoots but further back along the branch. More buds means more candles next year and more twigs the year after. Nevertheless, the majority of pines will be in training for four or five years before they begin resembling real bonsai. If you are not bulking up material, the appearance of bonsai pines as they progress in training can be greatly improved by carefully pulling out all of the needles growing underneath shoots, leaving only those above and to the sides of

branches. This exposes the undersides of the branches, a characteristic of full-sized trees.

Firs, spruces and larches have a similar growth pattern to pines, with several buds forming near the tip of each shoot. Pruning is similar, excess shoots being removed completely and the tips of others being twisted off according to their position on the tree. However, new buds for next year form as each shoot extends, so it is best to wait until you see several before pruning each shoot. Prune earlier than this and back buds may not form, leaving you no way of extending the branch next year.

The growth of conifers with compact, scale-like foliage such as junipers and *Chamaecyparis* is more spread out over the year; indeed it is not unusual for junipers to have been growing virtually all year in recent mild winters. These species require fairly regular pruning throughout the growing season, unless specific areas are being allowed to grow on. Pruning consists of simply twisting off the ends of shoots with the fingers (wear gloves for the junipers with needle-like leaves), taking the shoots of the apex back further than those lower down. Most scale-leaved conifers abhor the touch of metal, and cut shoots invariably brown around their edges, which looks unsightly. Twisting off shoots gives a cleaner break with less likelihood of browning. This group will actually bud back on to old wood, so keep an eye out for shoots forming in branch forks or on the trunk and remove as and when necessary.

With deciduous and broad-leaved evergreens, scissors can be used. Left to their own devices, such trees produce long, straight shoots while the aim in bonsai is to produce compact branches with short, twiggy growth. Maintenance pruning of areas not needed for extension, therefore, consists of tipping back emerging shoots as they are developing their first leaves. Removing the growing tip and last pair of leaves keeps the shoot short, that is, it reduces the size of the internodes and the wounding encourages the small buds in the leaf axils to develop. These then produce several side branches from the short original shoot, each of which can also be tipped back, producing more branching. Be selective on which side shoots you retain, and a pleasing branch structure can be obtained within a couple of growing seasons. This form of training, to encourage 'twigginess' or branch ramification, is central to producing the image of a full-sized tree scaled down. As before, the apex is pruned harder than the lower branches to equalize vigour.

While allowing the foliage 'clouds' of individual branches to fill out and adopt similar outlines to help unify the overall image of the tree, keep in mind the necessity to maintain the gaps between them. In most designs, these negative areas are central to maintaining the illusion of a mature tree. Overgrown bonsai can revert to a juvenile, amorphous mass of foliage, so regular pruning is as important as watering and feeding.

Repotting and soil mixtures

Potting, repotting and root pruning are central to bonsai, but there is no mystique involved. It is usually obvious when a tree requires repotting as it loses vigour and, as the pot is essentially full of roots, it dries out quickly. Trees in the early part of training and naturally vigorous types, such as willows and dawn redwood, require annual repotting, most other species every two to three years, and slow growers like pines can be safely left four or five. There are no hard and fast rules as it depends on the individual tree and the size and type of pot. The compost needs to be free-draining to give the roots enough air, moisture-retentive to supply the tree with water and able to hold enough nutrients to keep the tree fed.

There are almost as many compost recipes as bonsai growers, and several (rather expensive) specialist bonsai composts on the market. It is much cheaper to mix your own, however. A good all-purpose mix I have used successfully is two parts (by volume) peat-substitute potting compost (peat is also suitable, but harvested in environmentally damaging and unsustainable ways), two parts sharp-sand or lime-free alpine grit, and one part loam-based John Innes No. 3 potting compost. For ericaceous species such as azaleas, omit the John Innes as it contains lime and add an extra measure of soilless potting compost. Mix well, adding slow-release fertilizer, such as Osmocote, at the manufacturer's recommended rate if desired. The most common potting medium in Japan, an unusual granular clay called Akadama, is now available from specialist bonsai suppliers and although relatively expensive, gives excellent results. Pines like dry feet, and prefer acidic conditions so an extra measure of sand or grit instead of John Innes should be added to their compost.

The best time for repotting is undoubtedly spring, just as the buds begin to swell. Early autumn after leaf-fall is a better option for spring-flowering species, such as cherries, azaleas and crab apples, but protect newly repotted trees from frost. If potting a tree for the first time after initial styling, take it out of its pot, tease out the rootball as much as possible, scraping away the compost to expose the surface roots and reduce the rootball enough to fit it into a fairly large training pot. Cut off long and over thick roots so that the tree will fit into the pot. If it appears at all unsteady, thread a piece of wire over (or through) the rootball, passing both ends through the drainage hole in the base of the pot and secure firmly. It is usual to place the tree asymmetrically in the pot, not right in the middle.

Place the roots as radially as possible around the trunk and fill around them with your chosen compost, working it into the crevices between roots but not firming too heavily. Carry on filling up the pot but leave enough space below the rim to allow easy watering. Bonsai are often displayed with moss covering the surface, giving a passable imitation of grass around a full-sized tree, and this can be added at this stage – cracks in paving and shaded areas are usually good sources. Always water a newly potted tree, but do so gently to avoid disturbing the compost surface.

Repotting uses exactly the same procedure, but the tree will also need to be root pruned. Cut any retaining wire and ease the tree out of its pot. Gently and carefully tease out the rootball, which will probably be largely made up of roots running round and round the outside. Untangle them, and remove as much old compost from the outside of the rootball as possible. It is usual to cut around a third, up to a half, of the old roots of trees in initial training every year or every other year, depending on the vigour of the species (in the case of my dawn redwood, well over a metre of roots annually), giving plenty of room for fresh compost – and new roots. Older, fully-trained bonsai, and pines in particular, require much less frequent repotting, and are pruned less severely, a quarter of the rootball or less. If you are 'fattening up' trees in the ground, it is a good idea to undercut them every autumn using a spade to sever any roots growing straight down, which will encourage more root growth near the trunk.

Display pots

The choice of a display pot for a tree approaching its final form is largely a personal one. There are traditions and so-called 'rules' such as deep, rectangular pots for formal upright trees, shallow ovals for informal uprights and small, unglazed round pots for literati, but as with so much in bonsai, the rules and boundaries are continually being pushed and broken. Crescent-shaped artificial 'rock pots' are much in vogue at present for windswept and cascade trees, as are artificial slabs for group plantings. I would argue that the choice of pot is entirely up to the grower – if you like a pot's design or colour, and think it would suit a particular tree, use it. It used to be true that the best bonsai pots came from Japan, but this is frankly no longer the case. In Europe, in particular, native potters are producing beautiful work every bit as good as imported pots that are often cheaper, since the shipping costs from Japan are considerable.

Nevertheless, it is easy to make mistakes. The colour and finish of the pot should complement the tree, not clash with it, and the two together form a pleasing whole like a picture and its frame. Generally, coniferous trees are matched well to dark brown or grey, unglazed pots, and light, pastel-coloured or off-

Bonsai nurseries offer the best range of pots. Matching a tree with its final display pot is an inexact science and largely a matter of personal taste.

white pots look best with flowering trees where they will complement the blossom. The only colour that I always avoid is vivid, royal 'export blue'; it is called 'export' because it suits no species of bonsai, and no-one in Japan would entertain the idea of potting a bonsai into it.

Theft

An unfortunate side effect of bonsai's growing popularity has been an increase in instances of theft. Good bonsai are expensive, and the criminal fraternity has begun to recognize this. The monetary value of prized specimens is as nothing for a grower compared with the loss of a tree that may have been cherished and developed over many years; losing such trees has been likened to a bereavement. Anti-theft devices such as thick wires akin to bicycle locks that pass over or through the pot and rootball to secure trees to their stands are becoming more commonplace (including at RHS Garden Wisley), and trees can even be 'microchipped' by inserting a small chip into the trunk, like the identifying chips placed under the skin of many pet dogs and cats. Perhaps the most effective measures are to site your trees where they are not visible from outside the garden, installing a stout wooden fence or enclosing the garden with hedging, and keeping the garden gate locked at all times.

Conclusion

To sum up, I hope the text, but more importantly the pictures of some exceptional trees, in this book have inspired you to try your hand at creating and developing bonsai of your own, and given you a better idea of what makes a good specimen. For those of us really bitten by the bug, it is a captivating and rewarding hobby that can verge on the obsessional. It can also inspire a deeper appreciation of the characteristics and shapes of trees in general, in the wild and in cultivation, and of the passing of the seasons. If you find yourself stopped in your tracks while pondering the shape of mature trees, and wondering how to create the same images in miniature, you are thinking along the right lines. If your appetite has been whetted, the further information section (p.88) includes details of bonsai books, magazines and societies.

A bonsai display at RHS Wisley, including a magnificent Acer palmatum *'Deshojo' in the foreground. Note the anti-theft devices at the base of the trees.*

FURTHER INFORMATION

Some of the books I have found most useful in developing my interest in bonsai are detailed below. There is likely to be a local bonsai club in your area which can be an excellent source of information and inspiration and put you in touch with like-minded enthusiasts. Contact the Federation of British Bonsai Societues (FOBBS) for more details at: www.fobbs.co.uk Address queries to **fobbs.base@ntlworld.com**

The most successful magazine on the subject, called simply *'Bonsai Europe'*, is now published (in English) in the Netherlands and is genuinely pan-European. Published bi-monthly, it is available from bonsai nurseries (most of which advertise their details in it) or direct from Bonsai magazine subscription service, Int. Antwoordnummer 12300, 4040 ZX, Kesteren, The Netherlands. You can also subscribe on-line at: **www.bonsaimagazine.com.**

BOOKS:

The Art of Bonsai, Peter Adams, 1981, Ward Lock
Successful Bonsai Shaping, Peter Adams, 1993, Ward Lock
The Art of Flowering Bonsai, Peter Adams, 1998, Ward Lock
Bonsai Landscapes, Peter Adams, 1999, Ward Lock (Trained in
      Fine Art, Peter Adams is excellent on bonsai design
and the analysis of tree styling)
The Living Art of Bonsai, Professor Amy Liang, 1995, Sterling
      Publishing Company (Covers Chinese, Taiwanese and

Japanese beech trees are renowned for their exceptional autumn colour. There are many cultivars that are suitable for bonsai.

Japanese schools)

The Macdonald Encyclopedia of Bonsai, Gianfranco Giorgi, 1994,
Little, Brown and Company (Good for species profiles)

The Practical Guide to Growing Bonsai, Craig Coussins, 2001,
Apple Press (Aimed at beginners)

The Bonsai Book, Dan Barton, 1989, Ebury Press
(Quirky but useful)

Bonsai Life Histories, Martin Treasure, 2001, David and Charles
(Traces the development of individual trees)

Bonsai, Susan M. Bachenheimer Resnick, 1991, Harper Collins

Bonsai: A Hamlyn Care Manual, Collin Lewis, 1997, Hamlyn
(Practical and well-illustrated)

The Complete Book of Bonsai, Harry Tomlinson, US Edition (UK
unforgivably out of print)(The best book for the
beginner)

'DK Pocket Encyclopedia: Bonsai', Harry Tomlinson (abridged
version of the above in smaller format)

RECOMMENDED NURSERIES:

Nurseries I can recommend from personal experience include:

Heron's Bonsai

Wiremill Lane, Newchapel, Nr Lingfield, Surrey, RH7 6HJ
Tel: 01342 832657
Website: www.herons.co.uk

Greenwood Bonsai Studio

Ollerton Road, Arnold, Nottingham, NG5 8PR
Tel: 0115 9205757
Website: www.bonsai.co.uk

Banksia Bonsai

Chapel Lane, Southbrink, Wisbech, Cambs PE14 0RX
Tel: 01945 465176
Website: www.bonsaitrees.uk.com

Most bonsai nurseries offer a range of workshops and
demonstrations, which allow you to see trees being worked on

'in the flesh'.

SPECIES FOR NOVICE BONSAI GROWERS:

The following species of trees and shrubs all adapt well to pot cultivation and are relatively quick to develop and amenable to bonsai training. Space precludes describing them in more detail. Species marked with a star are not reliably hardy in most of the UK and will require the protection of a cold glasshouse or unheated porch in winter.

Flowering and fruiting species:

Cotoneaster species and cultivars, particularly *C. horizontalis*
Crabapples (*Malus* species and cultivars)
Hawthorns (British native *Crataegus monogyna* particularly)
Firethorn (*Pyracantha* species and cultivars)
Cherries and relatives (*Prunus* species, particularly small-leaved *P.mume* and *P. incisa*)

Conifers:

Junipers (*Juniperus* species and their cultivars, particularly *J. chinensis* and *J. rigida*)
Chamaecyparis lawsoniana and *C. obtusa*, particularly smaller and dwarf selections
Spruces (*Picea* species, particularly their dwarf cultivars)
Yews (*Taxus*, particularly British native *Taxus baccata* and *T. cuspidata*, Japanese yew)
Cryptomeria japonica

Although the majority of conifers are evergreen, several deciduous species are well-suited to bonsai:
Larches (*Larix* species. European *L. decidua* and Japanese *L. kaempferi* very similar)

Deciduous broadleaves:

★Trident maple (*Acer buergerianum*, Japanese species best suited to root over rock)
Field maple (*Acer campestre*, small-leaved European native)
Beech (*Fagus* species, particularly European *Fagus sylvatica* and Japanese *F. crenata*)

Hornbeams (*Carpinus* species, particularly European *C. betulus*)
Birches (*Betula* species)
The following are all also suitable for beginners, but often prove slower to develop and may require more care (such as winter protection from cold temperatures and wind) as some are not as hardy. They are better suited therefore to more experienced growers (or those with more patience to begin with).

Flowering:

Azaleas and rhododendrons (Japanese Satsuki azaleas, cultivars of *Rhododendron indicum*, *R. kiusianum* and alpine species such as *R. impeditum*. All require acid compost)
Wisteria species and cultivars
★Olive (*Olea europea*, evergreen, can adapt to indoor cultivation)

Conifers:

Pines (*Pinus* species, particularly *Pinus pentaphylla*, Japanese white pine; *Pinus thunbergii*, black pine; *P. mugo*, mountain pine and British native *P. sylvatica*. Require free-draining compost and patience)
Cedars (*Cedrus* species, particularly blue-needled *Cedrus atlantica*, Glauca Group; and dwarf cultivars of *C.libani*, cedar of Lebanon)
Firs (*Abies* species)
★Dawn redwood (*Metasequoia glyptostroboides*, fast-growing, and deciduous)
★Swamp cypress (*Taxodium distichum*, similar to above but even less hardy)

Deciduous broadleaves

Japanese maples (many *Acer palmatum* cultivars and varieties)
Oaks (*Quercus* species)
★Maidenhair tree (*Ginkgo biloba*)
★Chinese elm (*Ulmus parviflora*. Can be grown indoors but much prefers life outside in the summer)
★*Zelkova serrata*

Acknowledgements:

Illustrations: Patrick Mulrey
Copy-editor: Stella Martin
RHS editor: Simon Maughan
Proofreader: Rae Spencer-Jones
Index: Sue Bosanko

The author's sincere thanks are due to all the bonsai artists whose work is depicted in this book.

Trees by Harry Tomlinson, Greenwood Bonsai Studio, Nottingham (photographs by Tim Sandall): Cover and page (around 40 years, pot by Petra Tomlinson); Pages 21, 57 (35 years, Japanese pot); Page 23 (25 years, pot by Gordon Duffett); Page 26 (45 years, pot Korean); Page 27 (34 years, slab by Petra Tomlinson); Pages 28, 68 (15 years, pot Japanese); Page 35 (25 years, pot by Petra Tomlinson); Page 43 left to right, (18 years, pot Japanese), (12 years, pot Chinese), (12 years, pot Japanese), (28 years, pot by Petra Tomlinson); Pages 45, 89 (25 years, pot by Petra Tomlinson); Pages 63, 66 (30 years, pot by Petra Tomlinson); Page 71 (Trees by Harry and Petra Tomlinson); Page 72 (around 25 years, pot by Petra Tomlinson); Page 87 (25-30 years, pot by Petra Tomlinson).

Trees from the bonsai collection at RHS Garden Wisley, donated by Peter and Dawn Chan, Herons Bonsai, Surrey (photographs by Tim Sandall): Pages 6, 12, 18, 19 (top and bottom), 20 (top), 25 (top and bottom), 29, 30, 31, 33, 37, 47, 58, 75, 76, 78, 79, 81, 85.

Trees exhibited at the RHS Chelsea Flower Show 1998 (photographs by the author): Pages 2 and 20 (bottom left) Exhibitor unknown; Pages 15, 17 and 39 Bonsai Kai Society, London; Page 20 (bottom right) Herons Bonsai; Page 60 Federation of British Bonsai Societies.